# Northern Lights

# Northern Lights

*An Anthology of Contemporary Christian Writing in Canada*

Editors

*Byron Rempel-Burkholder*
*Dora Dueck*

John Wiley & Sons Canada, Ltd.

*Library and Archives Canada Cataloguing in Publication Data*

Northern lights : an anthology of contemporary Christian writing in Canada / [edited by] Byron Rempel-Burkholder, Dora Dueck.

Includes bibliographical references.
ISBN 978-0-470-15526-4

1. Christian literature, Canadian (English). 2. Canadian literature (English)—21st century. I. Rempel-Burkholder, Byron, 1957- II. Dueck, Dora, 1950-

BR53.N67 2008          C810.8'03823          C2008-902159-2

**Production Credits**
Cover design: Adrian So
Interior text design and typesetting: Michael Chan
Printer: Tri-Graphic Printing Ltd.

John Wiley & Sons Canada, Ltd.
6045 Freemont Blvd.
Mississauga, Ontario
L5R 4J3

The text pages of this book are printed with biodegradable vegetable-based inks on 55lb. recycled cream paper, 100% post-consumer waste.

Printed in Canada

1 2 3 4 5 TRI 12 11 10 09 08

**Mixed Sources**
Product group from well-managed forests, controlled sources and recycled wood or fiber
www.fsc.org Cert no. SW-COC-1352
© 1996 Forest Stewardship Council

# Table of Contents

# Introduction

This collection is an experiment in identity.

Its conception occurred almost by accident on a snowy March morning in Winnipeg, near the longitudinal centre of Canada. On his daily walk to the bus stop, Byron found himself mulling over the relationship between spirituality and geography. That connection had planted itself in his mind a decade earlier through American poet Kathleen Norris's memoir *Dakota*, a moving chronicle of Norris's rediscovery of faith upon her move from New York City to her grandmother's windswept prairie hometown of Pierre, North Dakota. How did living in Canada, he wondered, affect his own identity as a Christian?

Whether it was the snow or the barometric pressure of that winter day, the question stuck, and it spawned others. What is the spiritual geography of Canada? The country has many physical geographies—but what are the spiritual ones? And is there such a thing as a Canadian spiritual identity, or do we Canadians simply borrow from the habits, songs, writing, and preaching of our neighbours across the forty-ninth parallel?

A generation ago, university halls were abuzz with the discovery of a distinct literary landscape in Canadian novels and poetry. CanLit, as it was called, produced a rich body of reflection and a surge of exciting new writing to further delineate its contours.

But what of our spiritual landscape? How was it being mapped into words? And who were our spiritual writers and leaders?

That day Byron emailed Dora, another Winnipeg editor. Did these mullings, he asked, have any validity? And might Canadians be interested in a collection of writing that reflected the many faces of being Christian in Canada?

Dora was immediately intrigued by the questions and the idea of a book. In her journal that day, she began to jot words in the margin—words that seemed to adhere not only to the earth

but also to the soul of the northern half of this continent that
First Nations people have called "Turtle Island." North. East
and West. Cold and snow. Prairie, city, mountain. Vast.

☙

As we [Byron and Dora] brainstormed further, this margina-
lia expanded into a chart of words that juxtaposed Canadian
geography, history, sense of home, and emotional orientation,
with the broad spiritual themes of birth and incarnation, suffering and death, transformation and glory.

Another list—this one of possible contributors to an anthology—began to take shape over a series of breakfasts with
*ChristianWeek* editor Doug Koop, who offered his enthusiastic encouragement and extensive knowledge of the national
religious scene. After a string of meetings, emails, Internet
searches, and discussions with others, we had a proposal in
hand, and then a commitment from Wiley Canada to risk
publishing the collection. Byron and Dora would work as editors on the project; Doug would be the marketing contact.

We decided early on that this collection would be Christian rather than interfaith. The latter would have been just as
rich and would certainly have reflected the diversity of this
country. But as Christians nurtured by and familiar with our
own traditions, we felt there was also a compelling case for
gathering Christians from a broad range of heritage and experience around the theological narrative they share and call
"gospel."

Our aim was not to analyze, define, or argue about
Christian identity in Canada. Rather, we wanted to explore,
express, and showcase it. We wanted to discover it in a variety
of genres, from poetry to fiction, memoir to meditation. The
writing would come from literary figures, religious leaders,
public figures, and activists. Contributors would reflect the
many church traditions represented in Canada, from evangeli-

cal to Catholic, mainline Protestant to Orthodox, Pentecostal to Anabaptist. Some would still have family connections beyond our shores; others would have ancestors who were here long before the Europeans came.

This anthology is just a beginning of something that may continue to evolve. So we will be honest in our disclaimers. We did not include everyone who could have been included. Some declined our invitation for various reasons; others we learned about too late. We were unable to represent all regions as much as we would have liked, especially Quebec, and we were not equipped to make this a bilingual collection.

The writers we were able to bring together, however, are a wonderfully interesting and eclectic group, each one illuminating some important aspect of Christian faith and life in this country. For us, this project was a rewarding personal journey as we celebrated writers we already loved and discovered others we had not known before. The best part was reading all their contributions side by side. We were delighted with the mosaic that formed.

Does Canada have great writers who express what it means to be Christian in this country? The answer is an unequivocal yes.

And what of our spiritual geographies? They too exist and can be glimpsed, uniquely ours, and shaped by our land, our history, our people. The following pages take a look.

# Acknowledgements

Thank you so much to all the writers who agreed to appear in this collection—for your gift of good words; for your ideas, patience, and encouragement; and for friendships that resulted. In addition, many colleagues, friends, and media contacts have been generous with their interest, ideas, and help. Particular thanks go to Doug Koop, David Hunt, John Longhurst, Spencer Estabrooks, and Sister Mary Rose Hammerling.

We owe special thanks to editor Don Loney and the staff at Wiley Canada, whose enthusiasm and ongoing counsel have been so vital to this project's completion.

Finally, we offer our warmest gratitude to our spouses, Helmut Dueck and Melita Rempel-Burkholder. You have listened to us and cheered us on; you have put up with the project and walked alongside us from its beginning. We love you and thank you!

Dora Dueck
Byron Rempel-Burkholder

Dance to Creation

# Thirty Names
~ *John Terpstra* ~

In the land where we live
   there are thirty names for snow.
The stars are bright unfallen flakes, poured from a dipper.
The sun is the single star of God, melting our locked tongues.

In the country we inhabit
a chinook choruses down the choir loft of the Rockies,
   and frees the water locked in ice and snow.
The water hurls down the mountain,
   contemplates plain and prairie, muskeg and shield.
The rivers run and hustle,
   meander past oak and aspen, corn and bean,
   by treeline, trapline, lichen and moss.

A killdeer hurries across the sand,
   distracting the grizzly, come for salmon.
Squirrel and elk, rattlesnake and cattle,
   the walrus lolling on an ice floe,
   cod and narwhal, kingfisher, lobster and loon,
are neighbours in this land of water,
   water frozen and free;

are neighbour to the raven, a black crow,
   a murder of crows in the neighbourhood tree;

our neighbour is a rampant raccoon, lamprey eel, zebra
mussel.
Our neighbour is non-native, migrant, immigrant.
Our neighbour is Inuit, Ojibwa, Cree.
Our neighbour dances the Sun Dance, observes Hanukkah,
Ramadan,

the days of the Saints, Easter.
Our neighbour waits and watches, at the window,
   three thousand miles away.


In the land where we live,
we journey through white-out conditions to the fixed pole,
   the goal of our arctic expedition;
we swing and spin round a second pole, called magnetic,
   which changes position, confusing our compass.
As children falling in drifts and banks,
   we dream under northern lights,
singing Snowmaker, Icebreaker, who frees the waters,
Earthshaper, Poleshifter, True North of our yearning,
God of thirty names,
   thirty thanks, times three.
Amen.
   Again, more loudly:
Amen.

---

John Terpstra has published eight books of poetry, including *Two or Three Guitars: Selected Poems*. An earlier work, *Disarmament*, was shortlisted for the Governor General's Literary Awards. His poetry has won the CBC Radio Literary Prize, the Bressani Prize, and several Arts Hamilton Literary Awards. His memoir, *The Boys, or, Waiting for the Electrician's Daughter*, was shortlisted for the Charles Taylor Prize for Literary Non-Fiction and the British Columbia Award for Canadian Non-Fiction. He lives in Hamilton, Ontario, where he works as a cabinetmaker and carpenter.

# Here
~ *Susan Fish* ~

The place slips quietly, unexpectedly, into my life one summer. My sister calls to say she has bought her in-laws' cottage in the remote reaches of Quebec.

"You should come," she says. It sounds like a joke. We have three preschoolers and I have a tricky back. She explains that the cottage is on the south shore of the St. Lawrence River, four hours past Quebec City. She tells us to expect any kind of weather, including snow. We find ourselves packing the van with strollers, winter coats, and bathing suits, and then we drive for three days.

We arrive at low tide on a blindingly sunny day and stand on the bare beach. We cannot see the north shore of the river and it might as well be the sea. I feel slightly disoriented but victorious. The water is too cold for swimming, even in August, but it is salty and it covers the rocks twice a day, then uncovers them, revealing little worlds of wonder. The beach is full of sea glass in all sizes and colours—we can't take two steps without finding some—and we become instant collectors. One day we discover a live crab in a tidal pool, legs pedalling helplessly, before we put it back under its ledge.

Night falls early here and the children slip easily into dreams while we write, read, and do puzzles. We hear the morning before it arrives—shorebirds sing reveille at about four. If we aren't up by five-thirty, we feel like slackers, missing the day.

Neighbours greet us in French, English, and Dog. We discover that salmon, raspberries, and honey are local delicacies here and we devour them. We paint little stones on the beach one day and roast marshmallows another. There is nothing that must be done.

What we notice most is the air. Damp from the spray of the river, the air is so clear we feel our lungs expand. The sea-smells of salt and fish mingle with the tang of wild roses that grow along the beach, and with the scent of the fir and cedar that stand on rocks rising from the water. The little English school asks my husband to stay and teach—and though we decline, I am nearly ready to pack up my life and move here.

༄

I write poetry and prose about the place, like a lover seeking to capture the essence of the beloved. On the bulletin board behind my desk, I tack up a photograph of the river and imagine the place, snow dense and packed, stones slippery and capped with ice. We pretend we are walking the St. Lawrence's shores, that we have spotted whales. I display sea glass in jars, glue it onto frames, embed it in art and verse. Periodically on car rides, I take votes: who thinks we should just keep going till we reach the cottage? The delight is so deep, my enthusiasm must be kept private lest it embarrass me like some rampant patriotism.

༄

The second time, we know how to do the trip. I can trace with my mind's fingertips the mountain ridges signalling Rivière-du-Loup. There's Capitaine Homard's and the honey place too. Can we stop at the tourist centre to check the tides? Let's go to the good grocery store in Rimouski.

But familiarity breeds disappointment and we are fogged in for days, saturated with rain. At an art show in a neighbouring village, we see oils and acrylics of the Gaspé sky's many moods.

My own mood is equally fickle, uncertain whether this place will continue to draw us year after year or whether its charm was transitory. Exactly what made this place so special to us?

They say children demonstrate readiness to read when they add a horizon line to their drawings. Here the horizon smudges with fog and all perspective can disappear into heavy weather—so that we seem utterly alone in a landscape without form. But here too everything can sharpen into intense relief.

I start to write a novel about a man who arrives here as a tourist and agrees to stay as a teacher. Like a Michelangelo sculpture, he emerges from stone, carved by the winds, waves, and the people of the place.

I am not from this place. While this means I am oblivious to some realities, I also may see more here than locals do, and more than I could at home.

❧

I wake early here and have long conversations with God. I'm perpetually wrestling with God about the same thing or another, but here I listen for answers. Here where there are fewer distracting voices—no computer, no friends, no meetings, and only fuzzy French television—I laugh and play more. I shift from solving and striving into pondering and reflecting. I slow down to see and to smell and to listen.

We look hard for whales and make up a song about our quest: "Whales of the deep, where are you? We'll feed you krill, we'll pay the bill / Whales of the deep, where are you?" Once we saw a dead beluga, rocking in the surf along the shore, which tells us the whales are really out there.

And then, at last, they are here. There is no other way I would rather go blind, I say, sitting on a deck chair, eyes squinting through binoculars across brilliant sunlit water to the horizon, where tiny black crescents have been spotted. Mostly we see only their backs. But there is no mistaking the real thing and I cannot believe my delight.

Early this morning, a Bible reading from Hebrews 12 struck me as complicated. It urged me to fix my eyes on Jesus in order to be rid of all that weighs me down and entangles me. Now as I watch the whales, I suddenly think of this verse. We train our eyes on the horizon, looking for evidence, while the children play on the beach, semi-ignored. We invite other people over and crowds gather, thrilled, like those in the marketplaces and on the hillsides who hurried to see Jesus and didn't even care about their suppers. They sit with us, using our binoculars to see for themselves. We use language as precisely as we can so that others can see what we see—"There! Eleven o'clock. Do you see it?" Some of us survey the whole sea while others fix a steady gaze on the spot of the last sighting. Though our eyes ache from staring into the sunlight, we do not turn away or falter. We eat outside, our orientation always toward the water, so we don't miss the final arc of back and fin.

෴

At home, our children are busy with friends and programs, but here the relentless tide reduces life to bare elements and simple games. Our middle child has had a tough year at school, and I watch it fall away as he stands on a big jagged rock, yelling "Chicken!" to each boom and crash of wave. Our youngest crouches over tidal pools, more settled than at home, while our oldest is just full and glad. My husband unwinds here—he reads for hours and naps when his energy wanes. When he does elaborate jigsaw puzzles, I see the boy emerge from the man. We reconnect here and build fires.

I search out soap, jam, honey, knitted slippers, and paintings—made things, things where memory and place are tucked into stitch, stir, and stroke. I weave these products into my life at home as I blend the things that put me in my place—the things I discover when I search the horizon and sift the sand at my feet, the things I hear when the only sound is the surge and pull of wave against rock and sand, millions of stones drawn in a quiet sweep.

———————

Susan Fish lives in Waterloo, Ontario. She writes for various charitable organizations and publications, and is currently interim communications coordinator for Conrad Grebel University College of the University of Waterloo. Susan is author of the novella *Seeker of Stars*, three books of Bible study curriculum, and more than sixty published articles. She is at work on her third novel.

# Love and the Law
*~ Molly Wolf ~*

The days are closing in now. When I go for a long walk after
supper, it's always at least dusk, and sometimes almost dark,
when I finally cross the bridge down where the rivers meet, the
Gananoque emptying into the St. Lawrence. I stop there, listening to the water lap on the limestone boulders, looking over the
lessening crowd of rivercraft at the marina. Just for an instant,
a strip of sunlight breaks through the cloud cover and the water
comes alive with light, silver inlaid on pewter, streaked sharply
with shadows where the eddies curl around the rocks. It occurs
to me to wonder, as I never have before, about these stones.
Where did they come from? Who were they?

They're probably a mixture of the local limestone and stuff
that got dumped here long since by the glaciers. Compared to
the ferociously beautiful Canadian Shield, just to our north and
west, these rocks are young—a mere 500 million years (says
the Canadian Geological Survey), while the nearest bits of the
Shield are nudging their billionth birthday. Nonetheless, half a
billion years is definitely antique. They've been around far longer than the rivers themselves, these boulders. Now they lie in
the water being pounded and tumbled, blasted by the summer
sun, invaded by ice-fingers, banged against other stones. They
simply endure. You have to admire them for that.

Water seems so fickle by comparison—nothing you can
put your foot on with any safety. Water's patterns only *seem*
fixed and permanent; put a finger into a water formation that
looks like it was frozen in glass and it instantly breaks into a
different pattern. Water is soft stuff, slippery and unpredictable. Look at a creek, rising and falling with the seasons,
torrential in the spring runoffs and meekly sluggish in August,
variable and moody. I can pick up a handful of water and it
will run through my fingers, leaving my palm wet and empty.
What's that for someone to depend on?

Soft, maybe—but self-possessed. I cannot make water my own; it is, at best, only on loan to me for the moment. I cannot squeeze it or compress it or bend it to my will. You can't get a grip on water the way you can on a rock. You can control it to a degree, but not ultimately. It has its own laws, which are not yours, and it goes its own way, which may not be the way you want.

A rock, now that's a different matter. It's predictable. You can trust it; you know where you stand with it. You can build with rock; you can make things of it, make it your own, use it for your own purposes. Look at the town's grave handsome limestone houses, solidly based, feats of workmanship and propriety, of caution and forethought, strong and enduring. That's something to admire.

And of course, conversely, you can pick a rock up and throw it at someone's head, if you feel that the someone deserves it. Throw a handful of water and you won't get any respect, unless it's frozen water with a stone in the middle, and that's cheating.

Worse still, while you can't throw water, water can throw you. It can come thundering down, tearing everything before it; this country isn't subject to rockslides, but oh, how it can flood! Water is dangerously free. It sneaks up through the basement floor or down through a problematic roof; it sprays all over the joint when a pipe breaks. It ends up where you least want it and not where you do want it, while rocks just stay where you set them.

But looking at the rivers leaves absolutely no doubt which of the two, rocks or water, will win out in the end. There is no doubt which is the shaper, the motive force—which has the real power, which says "Go!" and which says "I must, because you make me go; where will I fetch up?" The water is an irresistible force. The rock is a moveable object, although sometimes it takes quite a while and a whole lot of persuasion for it to move. Ultimately, water will wear away even older and tougher rock than this.

So why, as I lean over the bridge's parapet and stare at that strip of silver water, why do those particular words come whispering into my mind: *Love and the Law?*

Because Love is the living water, and the Law is a good strong rock, a respectable rock, a worthy and ancient rock; but a rock is just a rock. You can set your foot on the Law and feel assured that it will bear your weight—but only if it's well-seated. Law, like a rock, can turn under your foot and send you sprawling if it's not soundly based, and then what use is all its hardness and solid definiteness? You can pick up the Law and hit someone else on the head with it, and feel strong and well-defended and full of righteous anger—and your victim will *always* have been asking for it, because you're a good person and good people only throw rocks at those who break the Law and deserve stoning. Yeah. Right.

But while the Law can't tumble you head-over-heels the way Love can, and it never takes you into interesting and dangerous places the way Love does, so the Law won't keep you alive in the desert places of the heart, as Love will. It won't nourish growth and life, as Love does. You *can* live without rocks. Try living without water sometime. You're like me and everyone else; 80 per cent water, as salty as the sea. I may and should build my house on rock instead of sand, but what will become of me without water? Certain death, and quick.

I know in my very bones that onrushing Love will tumble the Law arse over teakettle, like a rock in a creek's spring run-off, smashing what is weak and flawed, shaping it, refining and smoothing it, proving what is really sound and should survive, and pounding into gravel anything with a flaw deep in it—although sometimes the Law will look sound and whole until that flaw appears. I know that the Law must ultimately yield to Love, just as in however many years, these rivers will reduce these ancient rocks to gravel.

I know I cannot stand atop Love as though I ruled it. I cannot build my own dream house with it, or hug it to myself as a personal possession, or control who gets it, or throw it at someone's head in pride or vengeance.

But I also know that I can count on Love to bear me up and float me, if I'm willing to trust it and can see the power and deep order behind its apparent chaos. I can lie back in Love's arms and be held by it. I know it will carry me into and safely through white water, and float me into peace at the end. I know it makes me live. I know it will make me whole.

The living water of Love will be there when *all* the rocks—even the great grey handsome Shield—have fallen into the sun and are gone as though they never were. While the rocks were here long before the rivers that now shape them, they, and this earth, and the universe, and all creation from beginning to end, lie lapped in ever-flowing Love that started before the beginning of Time and will flow right out the other end of it.

We are called in the end to Love, not the Law. On this truth, I can stand more firmly than I ever could on the strongest, most ancient, most respect-worthy rock, knowing that however I set my foot, this soft unyielding firmness will not turn and let me down.

The last bit of light leaves; shadows deepen across the water and the cold creeps in. I pull my jacket warm about me and set out through the gathering darkness for home.

---

Molly Wolf is a freelance editor, indexer, and writer who lives with her three cats, Magnificat, Calvin, and Hobbes, in Gananoque, Ontario. She is a devout, if sometimes puzzled, Anglican and writes a weekly piece for email distribution called the Sabbath Blessing. Her books include *Hiding in Plain Sight*, which won the Catholic Press Association's award for Best First Book in 1998, and *White China: Finding the Divine in the Everyday*.

# The Song of the Paddle
~ *R. Paul Stevens* ~

At an international party outside Lijiang, the ancient Silk
Road crossroads of Yunnan Province, China, each person was
asked to sing a song from their homeland. Would we sing our
national anthem? After a brief conference, my wife Gail and I
decided on a canoeing song.

> My paddle's keen and bright,
> Flashing with silver...
> Swift as the wild goose flies,
> Dip, dip, and swing.

The song itself, which we both learned at Pioneer Camp
in Ontario as teenagers, has a rhythm evocative of the spiritual
journey. It was at that camp that my love for the Canadian
canoe and for canoeing was birthed. There I learned the
J-stroke, the draw, the circle stroke, and the Indian stroke—
that marvellous twist of the paddle so you never remove it
from the water but move forward soundlessly.

This amazing craft opened up our vast land of rivers and
lakes. One forty-pound canoe can carry two adults and a load
of gear, but it can be portaged over the head by one person
with paddles lashed to the thwarts to rest, uneasily to be sure,
on the shoulders. I have canoed rivers in several provinces and
territories—the Musquodobit (Nova Scotia), Rivière du Di-
able (Quebec), Petawawa (Ontario), North Thompson (British
Columbia), Nisutlin (Yukon); and scores of lakes—Molega,
Ponhook, Clearwater, Azure, Myrtle, the Bowron Chain—not
to mention salt-water canoeing on the mystical and misty west
coast of British Columbia.

Once, but only once, have I canoed with Mr. Canadian
Canoe, Bill Mason, a cinematographer and artist who gave his
life to embracing and expressing the beauty of the canoe and

its birthing country. I once canoed the Zambezi River in Zambia, above the Victoria Falls. Our guide warned us that the crocodiles below the surface were not to be a cause of worry as they were very intelligent and would avoid us. In contrast, he said, the hippopotamus would chop our canoe in half with bow and stern persons (my wife and I, to be specific) falling into the water: "Then you have to worry about the crocodiles." In a few minutes we ran into the behemoth himself. The guide, seeing I knew something about canoeing, said, "Does the name Bill Mason mean anything to you?"

"Yes, I have canoed with him." (I am not actually given to name-dropping but here I was ten thousand kilometres from home and amazed that someone, a Zimbabwean to be exact, would know about Bill.) "Well," said the guide, "he is the god of canoeing." Mason, a Christian believer, would have corrected him; he was a person whose faith was integrated with his love of canoeing and God's creation. He was a child enthralled before the grand beautiful show of a God who is beautiful. He believed in the spirituality of canoeing, as do I.

For one thing, canoeing is slow. And God is on a slow march. With faster and faster computers and speed boats that barely touch the water, canoeing is, in contrast, delightfully, sometimes painfully slow. Like the spiritual life itself.

Travelling fast we miss almost everything in the blur of speed. Canoeing along the water-etched rocky shore of Ruxton Island in the Gulf Islands of British Columbia, I see patterns in the sculptured rocks highlighted in the warm glow of the setting sun, the last sculpture of the day. Overhead an eagle watches us, evaluating the threat we represent. Trees erupt from unbelievably hostile rocky faces. Every rock is a riot of colours and textures if you travel slowly enough to see it. The dip, dip of the paddles and the drops of water off the blades synchronize with the squawking of the crows, gulls, and cormorants. In the distance a seal emerges, his whiskered

face pointed in our direction. He makes an assessment and
then disappears to emerge at an unexpected tangent. Beavers,
river otters, and the mighty moose can be seen from time to
time, and reverenced.

> Land of the silver birch,
> home of the beaver,
> where still the mighty moose
> wanders at will.
> Blue lake and rocky shore,
> I will return once more.
> Boom do de boom, boom.

For another thing, canoeing is the journey. And journey
is one of the metaphors of the spiritual life. There is movement toward a goal but like canoeing, the process is not for
the product; it is the product. John McPhee says in *The Survival of the Bark Canoe*, "A canoe trip has become simply a rite
of oneness with certain terrain, a diversion of the field, an
act performed not because it is necessary but because there
is value in the act itself." One engages in a spiritual journey
just as one climbs over the gunwales into the webbed canoe
seat, not to get somewhere but to be going. The spiritual
journey is not merely for the ultimate destination, whether
it be "spiritual marriage to God" or heaven, but to be more
fully aware of God, self, others, and creation. Not surprisingly, Jesus spoke of himself metaphorically as "the Way" and
his first followers described themselves with the same word:
people on the Way.

Canoeing is repetitive. Dip, dip, and swing. Mason called
this "the song of the paddle." Canoeing down the pure wilderness of the Nisutlin River in the Yukon as the drizzling rain
sneaked through my waterproof top and trousers, my son David asked, "Do you still hear the song, Dad? Or is it muffled?"

It's repetitive. It must be. Ten strokes on the left and
then ten on the right, with the bow person doing the same
on the opposite side. This is especially helpful when bracing
against a strong headwind. Lloyd, my canoeing buddy, and
I had climbed Wavy Ridge Mountain above Myrtle Lake. A
knee injury made him hike all the way down—backwards!
When we got to the lake it was absolutely still, as it had been
when we started before dawn, a perfect mirror. But halfway
across to our campsite, the mountain gave us its windy blast.
Angling into the waves, rotating left and right, being careful
not to ship water, but in perfect rhythm, we eventually made
it safely to the sandy point where hot tea and a warm tent
awaited us, and a dinner of canned chicken, fried onions, and
instant potatoes, five-star fare in the wilderness. One becomes
somewhat mechanical about this dip, dip, and swing thing. The
stern person adds a gentle turn on his or her J-stroke auto-
matically, without conscious thought, by keeping an eye on
the final goal.

My prayers with my wife each night before we go to sleep
are like this, repetitive. We pray for each of our children and
grandchildren by name, and something about the day. Very
repetitive. But life is repetitive. Every morning I get up and
read one chapter from the Old Testament, one from the New,
and a psalm, and then I take a long prayer walk down to Spanish
Banks in Vancouver. The same thing every day. But it is life-giving. We live not for the rhythm but through it. Just as we see not
with the eye but through it, as the poet Blake once said.

Fellow canoeists are soul friends. The repetition and the
slowness invite soul companionship. "When did you first
experience the warmth of God's love?" "What causes you to
celebrate?" "What gives you stress?" "What are the questions
you're asking at this point in your life?" "What are you struggling with in your relationships?" "How's your relationship
with God?" The coffee percolator throbs over the open fire

as the sun splashes its warm glow over the azure water, the mountains cramming heaven against both sides of the lake. Peter is fly casting and the magic of his amber line laces the sky in a poetic rhythm against this sublime canvas painted for us by the sun's last glow.

Yes, as the song says, "Blue lake and rocky shore, I will return once more."

---

R. Paul Stevens is Professor Emeritus of Marketplace Theology and Leadership, Regent College, Vancouver, British Columbia. He is the author of many books, including *Down-to-Earth Spirituality*, *Seven Days of Faith*, and *Doing God's Business: Meaning and Motivation for the Marketplace*. He is married to Gail, who canoes from the bow; they have three married children and eight grandchildren.

# Sit, Stay, Listen
*~ Hannah Main-van der Kamp ~*

> *... the world is essentially nothing other than divine speech.*
> —Tim Lilburn on St. Augustine

Vigorous but not frantic, a fox sparrow digs over her tiny rectangular patch, kicks wet sand backwards into the hole she's
just dug while clearing a new one. And so it goes. Blessed be
the scrabblers, labourers in dust-yards, diligent under grey
skies, for theirs is the kingdom of grubs and beach lice.

Without light shafts, but for the amber glow of her lower
mandible, the velveteen V's over her heart.

∽

One half of the cove is lit up, silver-plate flecked with glass;
the other, scratched glass. Sun's movements put the pattern
in slow reverse while tide steps closer in little pleats. Then
breezes send missives in contrary directions. At the water line,
tiny ochre carapaces scuttle this way and that.

Two shores, east and west, keep the cove stretched taut
between them, a long-term relationship, even though ravens
in opposition call each to each.

∽

Excise the mischief of hornets, pluck out thistles before they
seed, also elderberry (too tall). Root them out from the land
of the living.

We're making a natural woodland garden, re-disturbing
the disturbance of rawness, blasted rock, torn timber, and
concrete tailings on our building site.

How we labour to restore, hacking carefully around the
pearly everlasting, foxgloves, and a patch of goldenrod, seed-

ing unstable scraped slopes with clover. Rearranging chaos,
we whack away at that snake-in-the-grass, dewberry, that
sprawls as if it owns the place.

Not enough axes and chainsaws in the arsenal to negoti-
ate with alders. Around here, they're weeds. New cohorts
assemble in the dark, a phalanx we curse, our age-old burden.

❧

The inlet has no orifice for letting in noise, only a mouth
wide as a halibut's for inhaling clouds and streaky green eyes
to mirror air-sifting swallows, but no ears for the gravel pit
within reach of a shot where rock crushers and soil screeners
toil. The hillside is all growl but tide's tentacles only pick up
minute vibrations of scuttlers at its lip and the paddles of far-
off kayakers. Earthmovers groan but water turns a deaf ear.

Sit by its side and await the oracle, look look and your
ears become seers.

At the end of the day, the pit shuts up. A Saw-whet Owl
beeps its truck-backing-up beeps and then the bay opens its
hidden little ears just a crack.

❧

Cacophony in clover. Weeks and weeks to listen on bare feet
to bees, rounded white hum of surround sound. Evenings
under a dead tree, to await a solitary osprey. Its chill approach
whistle is homely as a mess of sticks.

❧

I set my hand to the plough, gas-fired weed whacker and
equivocate. Okay, we have to do it, clear a path to the beach
through waist-high ferns. Why? Those who have second
thoughts are not fit for what kingdom?

Because we are tenderfooted, because we must not take
bears by surprise, because every jungle needs a clipped edge.

So is it morally superior to chop down sword ferns manu-
ally with shears? Not to mention blackberry vines, their tearing claws with bloodied thorns?

Get it over with; the quickest way is the loudest; don't
procrastinate.

The old grove grows on thin soil over rotten rock. I get
out the nail scissors. A tree frog grips my hair.

❧

At the listening post for days, aural seeker, far from the bustle
of table chat, from the soothing opening of cupboard doors.
It cannot be taught, this labour of focused yet relaxed listening. Sometimes, in a pocket of woods' stillness, the spike of a
single note. Sit and stay even though the teacher may say nothing, maybe only a slight tremor, thread of a Hermit Thrush
sparse and shy.

Kinglets whisper dust motes.

Poet, columnist, and book reviewer, Hannah Main-van der
Kamp of Victoria, British Columbia, is an avid birder. Her
four volumes of poetry include *According to Loon Bay*. She con-
tributes regularly to both secular and Christian publications,
including *BC Bookworld* and the *Diocesan Post* (Anglican). Her
work has won several awards, including one from The Word
Guild. A founding member of Victoria's Imago Dei (contem-
platives active in the arts), Hannah teaches the reading and
writing of poetry as spiritual practice.

# Celestial Navigation
~ *Linda Hall* ~

It's our first extended trip out on the salt in *Gypsy Rover II,* our twenty-eight-foot sailboat, and my husband and I are naturally nervous. Just a bit. Me more than him, I suppose. The funnel-shaped Bay of Fundy, whose tides can reach up to forty-five feet at the head, is not to be taken lightly, especially by a tiny sailboat with two fairly inexperienced sailors.

Our first hurdle is the Reversing Falls. Have we calculated the slack water times correctly? Did we remember to figure in daylight savings? The Falls is a narrow channel that separates the St. John River, with its three hundred miles of navigable fresh water, from the Bay of Fundy, with its extraordinary, tourist-drawing tides. At high tide the water surges into the St. John River and at low tide it gushes back out again as the Bay empties into the Gulf of Maine and the Atlantic Ocean. There are four fifteen-minute periods of slack water per day, and we have studied the tide and current charts until we have dog-eared the pages and memorized the information. We hope we have it right.

We breathe a sigh of relief when we arrive at the Falls and, instead of churning dangerously, it is as calm as a mill-pond. The afternoon sun shines down on us, a huge yellow smiley face in the sky as we motor easily through.

As soon as we round the channel and enter the major and very busy Saint John Harbour, however, the fog is like a wall. Literally. It is a wall. A grey curtain of cold mist extends from as high up as we can see and ends at the grey water around our boat.

It's choppy, but that could be from the tugboats and the tankers, all ships we can't see. Quickly we flip on our radar and make contact with Fundy Traffic, the traffic controller of the harbour. Carefully following our radar, our GPS, our compass, our paper charts, and radio communication with Fundy

Traffic, we make it through. I am exceedingly happy when we are finally well away from the shipping lanes.

A couple of hours later the fog is still viscous, but there is nothing around us, and Rik, tired, heads down below into the cabin for a nap. Our destination is Dipper Harbour, a fishing cove some four hours away. There we'll tie up to a fishing boat for the night, borrow a mooring, or drop an anchor. When we get there we'll figure out what we'll do.

I am alone, outside at the helm, when I receive a gift. There isn't really a whole lot for me to do. Since what little wind there is, is blowing directly on our bow, we're motoring instead of sailing. The engine is humming nicely, the autopilot is engaged and steadily following our compass course, and the radar keeps me apprised of anything around. All I have to do is look at the gauges every so often and scan the horizon to make sure we don't hit anything the radar can't pick up, like a log. Hunks of streaming seaweed are also a problem. They can wind themselves around boat props, requiring underwater trips in frigid water. Fishermen say the Bay of Fundy has two temperatures: cold and bloody cold.

The fog lifts slightly and I watch the lacy, tatted edges of the waves as they white-cap around us. Occasionally a seal raises its dog head and looks over at me. I delight in sea animals, the dolphins that play in the water beside us, the seals. It's too foggy to see whales, but I know they're out there. I keep looking to the right for glimpses of land through the fog, see none.

It hits me then, our smallness. We are a mere pinpoint of humanity out on a powerful ocean. We are barely noticeable on the radar of large ships. Probably they would not see us at all. It becomes our job to keep away from them. It strikes me in a corny way that even though we're far from shore, I'm still on God's radar screen. And I smile at the thought while a couple of gulls screech overhead. In years past Rik and I and

our children have spent many a camping trip with my parents.
When nights got late and silly, the four of us, along with my
father who was a minister until the week he passed away,
would come up with "cheesy sermon illustrations." This would
qualify, I think. I'll have to remember it.

But it catches in my throat when I realize it's true. I wonder at the psalm: "When I consider your heavens, the work
of your fingers, the moon and the stars which you have set in
place, what are human beings that you are mindful of them,
mortals that you care for them?" (Psalm 8:3–4)

The fog begins to dissipate, but it doesn't lift from the
horizon, it rises from the centre. The sun glistens down on
our small craft, while all around fog rises and falls like wispy
dancers. Then the light, in little fingers, begins creeping in
underneath the edges of the fog. The effect is magical. I put
my hand to my mouth and wonder how it is that I am here and
a part of this.

Since I was small the ocean has been a wonder to me. I
could sit on the shore for hours, hugging my knees. I always
felt that if I looked long enough I could see to the very edge
of the planet. The sea held mysteries, and if I watched long
enough, maybe I would even learn some of them.

I glance at the GPS now and note our latitude/longitude
as we move along in a great circle of sea and sky, and I ponder
the perfectness of this universe. This GPS, which tells us where
we are by radio signals off satellites, is a fairly modern innova-
tion. It has been used in nautical travel for a little more than a
decade and is now becoming standard in cars. For hundreds of
years, however, sailors relied on the rather odd-looking triangular
instrument called the sextant to find their way across oceans. We
have one aboard our boat, a hundred-year-old handcrafted one in
a wooden box above our port settee.

Rik and I spent one year studying Celestial Navigation,
a difficult course, one that consumed my entire life for that

year. I've always been more of a literature person than a math person, and so learning the triangulations and advanced calculus this course required was a stretch, but a good one. Because it taught me about God.

There is a God-perfection in each blade of grass, every drop of water, every spider's web, but there is an even vaster beauty in the mathematical arrangement of the universe. Noting the exact time and the date, it is possible by aiming a sextant at the moon, or the sun, or a planet or star, and then doing some lengthy calculations, to figure out exactly where you are. When I learned that this was possible, all I could say was, Wow!

We change course a few degrees and head toward Dipper Harbour, and I recognize that my personal navigator is this One who has placed the dancing, dissipating fog around me. The One who set these tides in motion, who cast the stars into the sky, not in some random pattern as I might if given a handful of confetti, but in a perfectly ordered arrangement. The same God who keeps me on his radar screen, not as a tiny blip off to the side, to be ignored or skirted around, but right in the centre. My personal navigator is a God who desires a relationship with me, and every once in a while gives me a tiny view into his mind.

---

Linda Hall is an award-winning mystery writer. Her latest novel—of fourteen so far—is *Shadows at the Window*, the second in a romantic suspense trilogy. *Steal Away* and *Sadie's Song* were both nominated for Christy Awards and *Dark Water* was awarded Best Christian Mystery/Suspense Novel in Canada for 2006 by The Word Guild. She and her husband Rik live in New Brunswick and love to sail.

# For the Love of Trees
~ *David Waltner-Toews* ~

### 1. White Pine, Douglas Fir, Yellow Cedar
(Canadian White Pine Sawmill, Vancouver, Fraser River, 1970)

They weigh heavily against our hooks and chains,
these avuncular, waterlogged Gandhians,
sulking in the sloshing flotsam.
The union steward is telling me,
in his stalwart Anglo-Dutch,
I should read Kropotkin.
He is thinking about workers,
better pay, guys at the pub, a TV.
I am considering ecology,
mutual aid, trees, co-evolution,
how far from this mephitic fog
the creaking silence,
the prickly blue-green shrug
of a wind-blown branch,
the soft-headed moss.
Behind us, bark dishevelled,
the old tatterdemalions
scream with the band saws,
karaoke blues from hell.

They are just trees,
after all, I tell myself. This is not family.
At the green chain, my shoulders ache
from yanking them, resisting,
away from the glare and clattering steel
onto the cool stacks
in the dark behind me.

## 2. Maple, Aspen, Fir
(South Cape Chin, Niagara Escarpment, 2000)

The wooden furniture creaks,
falls silent.
Does it accuse?
A table. A pencil. A roof over my head.
A door.
Out there, gnarled roots cling
to rocks along the escarpment
clawing up the precipice
leaning out, giddily,
into the spray, gathering in hollows
along the crest. Roots unclenched,
they topple across my path.
My body returns, again and again
to that quiet breathing,
the life-giving *sotto voce* sigh,
the light patter of sun and rain
drizzling from the canopy.
I cannot get enough of walking
among the trees,
their thoughtless, perfect love
that holds,
and lets me go.

## 3. The craft

Oh sacred grove, now wounded,
what can requite thy worth?

Word, grooved with caring hand to word,
a craft to bear us, earth to earth.

David Waltner-Toews is a veterinary epidemiologist, essay-
ist, poet, and fiction writer. He is the founding president of
Veterinarians without Borders–Canada, and of the Network
for Ecosystem Sustainability and Health. Besides many scholarly papers, he has published half a dozen books of poetry, an
award-winning collection of short stories, a murder mystery,
and four books of non-fiction. The *Globe and Mail* has called
him a "genuine polymath." When not working abroad, he lives
in Kitchener, Ontario.

# Dancing the Rubber Ice
~ *Ralph Milton* ~

Am I just sentimental? Or is it true that spring on the prairies is more passionate and fun?

I live in the Okanagan Valley now, where springtime kind of seeps in slowly underneath the door. On the prairies, springtime comes like that! BAM! You shovel out a snowstorm one day, and the next there's balm upon the breeze. The swift seduction of a prairie spring sweeps you away with a warm and passionate kiss—loves you quickly into summer and is gone. A short, surprising love affair with life.

When spring hits the prairies, it thaws. Wow! Does it thaw! The sloughs fill up and the ditches run full, and children quickly trade their winter long johns for gumboots and go looking for rubber ice to dance on.

Do you know what rubber ice is?

It only happens in a slough or a hollow where the water is exactly one inch deeper than a nine-year-old boy's rubber boots. It happens overnight. A thin, plastic layer—not like ordinary ice. Rubber ice is flexible and, well, rubbery.

Adults have no idea what to do with rubber ice. But a child knows. You have to dance it.

⁓

I am nine years old and I can dance. One slow and lingering step and I can feel the ice sink slightly, sending snaps and crackles detonating through the slough. I have nine-year-old skill and nine-year-old rhythm, and the keen mind I lost when puberty came with its new kinds of challenges.

I am nine and I know this dance. I test the ice with each slow step, and know exactly when to move just as the ice begins to crack. Quickly, not too fast, a gliding slow ballet—always moving forward because to stop, even for a second, is to break the ice. Nor can you go back to ice you've danced before, because it is weak. But there is always lots of future—lots of ice to draw you on, dancing, moving forward just at the moment when the ice begins to sink beneath your feet.

I get a little braver—stay a little longer in each spot. My dance slows as I dare the ice to break, push the edges of my springtime passion, test the boundaries of my boyhood.

And the ice will break. Eventually, it always does. And I run, wet and shivering and defeated, to my mom, who dries me off and scolds me softly and talks about pneumonia.

"Aw, Mom, my feet aren't even a teensy bit cold. It's boiling out there."

There is gentleness in my mother's scolding. And sometimes just a hint of laughter. I think maybe Mom remembers rubber ice when she was nine.

꩜

Spring on the prairies is a quick, passionate love affair with life. Rubber ice to dance on, swimming holes to freeze in, feet to go barefoot on. Then spring is gone and the hot summer is upon us. Time to get to work. Time to live a thing called hope.

Those who farm the dry and unforgiving prairies know about hope.

Yes, hope.

Not bloody-minded positive thinking. Not gritting your teeth and toughing it out till the economy improves. Not even optimism. It's embracing the glory, the passion of life, and accepting the crud that infects it. And the pain. Springtime has taught you that you will break through and your boots will fill up—but not to dance the ice is to deny the gift of life with all its pleasure and its passion and its pain. To refuse the springtime teaching of rubber ice is to say "no" to summer hope.

Hope, real hope, is deeper than mere optimism. It's not at all like cranking up a positive attitude. It's not the phony "power-think" of real estate salespeople. There's nothing Pollyanna about it. You can't describe hope, or teach it, but you can see it sometimes, and you can live it.

I've seen hope in the swollen belly of my daughter when she bore our grandchild. I've seen hope in the face of a tired street worker showing a broken woman where she can get a bit of rest, a sense of safety, and a shower. I've seen hope in the eyes of a friend dying from cancer—convinced her life would not end when her body died. I've seen hope in the wrinkled face of my grandmother who lay on her bed and told me, "I'm just waiting for my Jesus."

I experience hope every time I plant a seed or tell a story to my grandchild or sit with Bev, my mate of fifty years, and hold her hand and listen to the heartbeat of our life, and remember how we've danced the rubber ice together.

I know about hope because as a small boy I learned to dance the rubber ice and feel the passion of a prairie springtime. And I found a "mom" that I could run to in my prayers—a Mother who danced the rubber ice and showed me something of the face of God.

---

Ralph Milton is a retired writer and broadcaster whose career has taken him all over the world. He has written more than a dozen books, among them *Angels in Red Suspenders*, *Julian's Cell*, and *The Spirituality of Grandparenting*. He has received two honorary doctorates and is a co-founder of Wood Lake Publications. Ralph is married to the Rev. Beverley Milton. They live in Kelowna, British Columbia, near their grandchildren in whom they delight.

# A Place in the World

## Miss Morley's Parrot
~ *Hugh Cook* ~

One of the defining moments of my life—frightening to me
since I was only seven—occurred as I stood on a dock in the
Coal Harbour waterfront of Vancouver, British Columbia, on
February 28, 1950. It was West Coast winter weather, foggy
with a chill in the air. Our family had arrived in Vancouver
only a day earlier after emigrating from the Netherlands,
landing at Pier 21 in Halifax and crossing 4,000 miles of the
country by train, and now here I stood, seven years old, on a
waterfront dock in a completely strange city. In order for you
to understand the import of what happened on that dock in
Vancouver, however, I need to go back to what my life was
like before our family immigrated.

I was born in 1942, the middle year of World War II, and
the earliest memories I have are of the war. They are characterized by fear—fear when the air raid sirens blew, starting
low and rising in pitch and volume so that the sound seemed
to drill right through me and I thought the world might end
and my mother would close the heavy brown velour curtains
of our living room windows to shield even as little as the light
of candles or oil lamps from enemy airplanes. Fear when we
learned that German soldiers with their rakish helmets and
bayonets were in the street below and my father would dash to
the bathroom upstairs and wriggle into a shallow secret com-
partment the size of a coffin under the bathroom's linoleum
floor and my mother prepared herself to tell the lie that her
husband was away even though any soldier stepping into the
living room would have known a man lived in the house from
the lingering odour of the Dutch cigarettes my father smoked.

My father owned a dairy products store on Appelstraat a
twenty-minute walk away from the North Sea, and on summer days after the war ended I carried my shovel and pail
and trekked through the sand dunes pocked with wartime

cement bunkers and down to the beach, where my mother
held a towel in front of me while I shimmied into my black
one-piece bathing suit with straps that came over my shoulders. I built sand castles and dug moats in the wet beach flats
and occasionally ventured into the frigid waters of the North
Sea whose shocking salt taste, when a wave snuck up on me
and I swallowed a mouthful, I still remember today. My father
would not be at the beach with us for he would be in the store
selling milk and eggs and bulbous balls of Edam and Gouda
cheese sitting ceremoniously in rows on wooden shelves after
my father had taken them from their rectangular wooden
boxes, and my brothers and sister and I would chew the wax
the cheese came wrapped in and pretend it was chewing gum.
Eggs came to the store in flats from the farm and when my
father discovered a cracked egg he would not discard it but
would lean back his head and tip the raw egg into his mouth
and swallow it whole—we had just come through the Hunger
Winter of '44 when people ate tulip bulbs, and we'd learned
not to waste food.

   We were *Gereformeerd* (Reformed), which meant that twice
each Sunday we walked to church, where people paid a sum of
money annually to reserve a seat, and five minutes before the
service began a little red light went on and people who stood
in the back could take any of the unoccupied seats, then during
prayers the men would rise and the women and children remain
seated and I would settle in for a three-point, forty-minute
sermon delivered by a *dominee* who wore a long black toga, and
on Sunday evenings when I'd become old enough to go I would
lean my head and gradually fall asleep against the satiny fox-fur
stole of my mother's coat while my father sat apart from us in
a front pew reserved for the church elders and the fox's snout
on my mother's shoulder grinned ferociously inches above my
ears. We sang the intricate long-note, short-note rhythms of
the sixteenth-century Genevan Psalms of Maître Pierre and

Louis Bourgeois which have been so loved by Dutch Reformed people, the result, 350 years later, of John Calvin's decree that Reformation churches sing the Psalms. My earliest encounters with Dutch language and poetry and spirituality find their confluence in these Genevan Psalms.

We were *Gereformeerd,* and therefore "people of the Book," a reality I experienced during my childhood in the Old Testament stories my father read at the supper table every day. On the one hand these stories were historical-redemptive stories of the faith, but they were also what fairy tales are to children, for they contain the same enchantment and magic and witchcraft and bloodthirstiness and undercurrent of sexuality that fairy tales have. A donkey speaks; an axe head floats on water; an evil king visits a witch's hovel in the night in order to speak to the spirit of a dead prophet; a painted, wicked queen is thrown from a tower so that her blood spatters against the stone wall and the horses' hooves; a king stands on his palace roof spying on a naked woman and then has sex with her before arranging her husband's murder. Thus I was read to by my father every day. What I wish to underscore here as a writer is that my earliest childhood experience of the power of poetry and narrative trace back directly to my Reformed community's tradition of singing Psalms and reading Old Testament stories. Music, literature, and worship were inextricably intertwined.

My father, always a man of principle, could not stomach the government bureaucracy and black market practices prevalent in Holland after World War II, and so he and my mother decided we would emigrate to Canada, specifically Vancouver. We packed our belongings in a huge wooden crate, took whatever money we were allowed to take out of the country, and left Holland mid-February 1950. We were to take a ship to London, England, travel by train to Liverpool, and there board *The Empress of Canada* for Halifax. I recall the embraces and tears on the pier at Hoek van Holland, and the slow, momentous movement of the ship away from the dock as we stood at the railing returning the waving of white hand-kerchiefs that grew gradually smaller and smaller till we could no longer see them, nor the people waving them, until finally the pier itself disappeared. With it disappeared the only world I had known.

In Halifax, we boarded the CPR and rolled through the Maritimes, Quebec, and southern Ontario, and during a three-hour stop at Union Station in Toronto my mother had my brothers and me get a haircut so that we could make a good impression on arrival, then on we travelled across the snow-covered prairies, the train's windows blackened by coal soot, the doors between the railroad cars crusted with ice. In western Alberta the train took on an extra locomotive to help us climb the Rocky Mountains, then it was down the other side to a hissing, clouds-of-steam halt in Vancouver.

We were housed in the grimy heart of Vancouver in a large room with high, green walls in a stone building known as the Immigration Home, whose basement contained jail cells holding AWOL merchant seamen. On the street I smelled the stench of inner-city grime and bacon and eggs coming from shabby restaurants and saw pigeons bobbing on the sidewalk and electric trolley cars and more Oriental people than I had ever seen, but what I did not see was *anyone* wearing the knee-length woolen plus-fours and argyle socks my mother had bought my brothers and me in Holland. We may have been immigrants just off the boat, but we were not stupid—we refused to wear the plus-fours.

Now this is what I was coming to when I began: a day or so after we arrived, I recall standing alone on that wooden dock on the Vancouver waterfront. Grey water sloshed against the creosoted pilings while a West Coast winter fog prevented me from seeing the omnipresent seagulls but whose sharp mewing I could hear—and what struck me suddenly like a blow to the solar plexus was the realization that if someone were to step into my little cocoon of fog at that moment and start speaking to me, *I had no language anymore.* I would not understand a word that person said and I would be mute, unable to speak. It was as if everything I had experienced, everything I had known, everything I might have wanted to tell someone, had been taken from me. I felt alien and alone. Even today, more than fifty years later, I experience the same feeling of loss when I read or hear the Dutch language used beautifully, particularly in Dutch poetry or Dutch humour, and I feel a keen sense of regret that I do not know my first language better, as if it were a child I have had to give up for adoption and no longer know, and with whom I now may make only occasional strained visits.

Many years later in a conversation I had with my mother, something she said helped me to understand the significance of that moment when I stood in my plus-fours on that wooden dock in the fog. I asked her what one thing, all these years later, she regretted most about immigrating. What I expected her to say was: close relatives we never saw again, or having had to give up our store in the Hague, or amenities she'd had to do without in order to send us children to Christian day schools and then to university. What my mother said, however, took me by surprise. "The one thing I regret most," she said, "is that I don't have my own language anymore so that I can't joke."

After my mother said these words I realized that the import of what I felt on that dock in my seven-year-old, naive and inchoate way, and which I would only later begin to understand, is what we have all come to know, namely that language is knowledge, language is culture, language is identity—or, as Margaret Atwood points out in *The Hand-maid's Tale*, that to be deprived of language is to be powerless. Immigrants know this sense of powerlessness. Language, as my mother implied, contains the subtle nuances upon which not only all humour, but all *meaning,* is based. As a writer I understood then another important lesson, namely that what my mother and father had bequeathed to me was not only a Dutch Reformed tradition of Psalms and Old Testament stories, but also a passionate interest in language, the vehicle of poetry and narrative, all of which coalesced in my becoming a writer. My mother, a first-generation immigrant who had had no schooling beyond grade six, never really developed the facility with English to enable her to express her sense of wit, a sacrifice she made while I, second generation, would learn a new language that became the medium for me to tell the story of the Dutch-Canadian immigrant experience. But if language is indeed knowledge and culture and identity, relinquishing my Dutch language meant that I would have to acquire new knowledge, confront a new culture, and forge a new identity.

If Appelstraat in Holland was the locus for my first seven years as Hugo Kok, my life in Canada as Hugh Cook goes back to Morley Street in Burnaby, where my parents bought a house for $7,500 three years after we'd landed in Canada. Morley Street was still semi-rural then, a short, dead-end gravel street that was a self-contained little community of a dozen houses, a highway at one end and bush at the other. If the street was a microcosm of Canadian society at large I knew we had moved to an interesting country. Across the street was Gus Dietrich, whom I admired because he drove bulldozers. Diagonally across from us were the Barkers, whose house stood behind tall evergreens and whose two kids we were not to play with—or rather they were not to play with us, for the family were Jehovah's Witnesses and were recluses who hid behind their tall cedars. More interesting to me was Rev. Mackay down the street, an elderly retired Presbyterian minister who also happened to be a nudist. Apparently he went without clothes inside his house, but working in his yard outdoors he bowed to public decency by wearing a blue loincloth similar to the ones Indians wore in Hollywood movies, the skin of his leathery torso tanned and weathered. I was puzzled by Rev. Mackay, for the only ministers I had experienced until then were Dutch *dominees* who wore black togas in church and preached long sermons and taught me catechism—now here was a minister who went around naked! I couldn't fathom that. I had seen photographs in the *Vancouver Sun* of the Russian Doukhobors in the Kootenays, whose zealot Sons of Freedom protested government interference in their lives by taking off their clothes—women included—and torching their homes and dynamiting schools, but Rev. Mackay dressed in a skimpy blue loincloth picking raspberries or hoeing a flower bed did not strike me as the sort to blow up his home. Reclusive Jehovah's Witnesses, nudist Presbyterians, Doukhobor arsonists—I knew we Dutch Calvinists must have been a strange lot in the eyes of Canadians, but we had nothing on some of the others.

The person our family was closest to was Miss Morley next door, a single elderly woman whose grandfather the street was named after. Miss Morley was a large woman, the grey hair in her bun tight as a knot in a wet rope; thick grey hairs sprouted from moles on her chin. She usually wore blue denim overalls covered with an apron made from gunny sacks and lived in an old house identical to ours, except it had not experienced my father's compulsion to remodel; whereas our house was now yellow and maroon siding, hers was an ugly brown glass stucco, nor did she have an interior stairway to the basement such as my father built, so we would see Miss Morley every day, slowly making her way down the slippery back stairs, when it rained, to feed the twenty Red Hampshire chickens she kept for eggs. If she was sick I would have to feed the chickens for her, and I would step into her dark, spider-webbed cellar with a dirt floor for the chicken feed and water. Once a week Miss Morley's brother would stop by to mow her lawn.

The most interesting thing about Miss Morley, however, was that she had a parrot, a blue and green macaw named Polly, which she kept in a cage in her kitchen, and on warm summer days when all the windows were open we could hear Polly's screeches split the air. I'd never seen anything as exotic up close as Miss Morley's parrot: the top of its head was a brilliant red sheen, the area around its eyes was also streaked with red, which gradually turned bright green on its back and the top of its wings, then an electric blue on its stomach. Its long tail feathers were a shimmering blue and red. I did not often enter Miss Morley's house, whose brown wallpaper and wood furniture and carpeting seemed as old as she, but whenever I did, Miss Morley, knowing why I had come, would lead me to the kitchen to meet Polly. The round stub of Polly's small, leathery tongue bobbed up and down inside its beak, then the bird would eye me from inside its cage with piercing eyes. The bird struck me as being infinitely more interesting than the yellow budgie named Pickles my mother kept in a cage in our kitchen.

These were the inhabitants of Morley Street, whose lives were to us as odd and eccentric as ours must have seemed to them. From these neighbours I learned still another equally important lesson for writers, namely that the mystery and complexity and staggering variety found in human lives exists not far away but on our very own street, next door, under our noses, lives as luminous as our own if we will but open our eyes.

Recently when I was out West I made a point of visiting Morley Street. I don't always like to do so, for I feel a stranger there now; it does not seem like the street where I played touch football with friends and built a fort in the bush and stole grapes from an arbour beside Rev. Mackay's house.

A few familiar houses from long ago still stand, old and dingy compared to the new homes meticulously landscaped with rhododendron and juniper and Japanese red maple. Our old house no longer exists, torn down to make way for two new houses, large two-storey white stucco homes with red clay roof tiles. Rev. Mackay's house has also been torn down. Miss Morley's house still stands, though Miss Morley passed away some years ago.

I do not know what happened to Polly—parrots have an amazing longevity, up to a hundred and twenty years, so that they often outlive their owners and are passed on to a son or daughter. My father and mother have also both died, yet the Reformed tradition which they passed on to me, a tradition of Old Testament story and Genevan psalm, of vigorous intellectual pursuit and cultural engagement, this tradition still lives, rich and vivid as the red and blue feathers of a parrot.

---

Hugh Cook's stories have appeared in Canada's leading literary journals. He has published three books of fiction: *Cracked Wheat and Other Stories*, *The Homecoming Man*, and *Home in Alfalfa*. In 1997 The Word Guild awarded Hugh the Leslie K. Tarr Award for outstanding contribution to the field of Christian writing. He is presently retired from teaching at Redeemer University College and lives in Hamilton, Ontario.

# Why I Enjoy My Job
~ *Douglas Todd* ~

It's expected in Canada that we have passionate opinions about movies, politics, crime, restaurants, and especially our hockey teams. But it's not stylish to have convictions about the ultimate nature of reality: about metaphysics, about cosmology, about theology.

In other words, it's not cool to be "religious" in Canada.

When it comes to foundational spiritual beliefs, the safest stance here is to avoid taking a stand. Institutional Christianity? Most Canadians say "forget it" and stay away in droves. Islam? Too heavy. Sikhism? A little odd. Judaism? Okay if you're Jewish. Buddhism? Well, the Dalai Lama seems a nice guy, but why do Buddhists surround their statues with oranges and incense?

In much of this country, especially in my home province of British Columbia, the most that many people can say about religion is to acknowledge they sort of feel "spiritual" when they're walking in the forest, doing yoga, being sexual, taking in a sunset, or skiing in the mountains.

Only 32 per cent of Canadians show up once a month or more at a religious institution, a figure higher than in most European countries but much lower than in the United States. As a result, the complex worldviews associated with ancient religions, and the valuable debates that have taken place within them for centuries, no longer receive wide airing in this country.

You can imagine how far a conversation about metaphysics, the study of the bedrock nature of reality, goes among my clever friends at the *Vancouver Sun*, where I've been writing about spirituality and ethics since the early 1990s. Good-natured teasing is the typical office fashion among journalists on religious topics, as it is in most Canadian workplaces.

And don't get me going on why courses on metaphysics,

also known as speculative philosophy, aren't offered in our public colleges and universities. Metaphysics could be taught without indoctrinating students. But most academic philosophers avoid it because their colleagues judge it anachronistic and unfashionable; they fear they could hurt their careers by showing serious interest in ultimate matters such as those surrounding beauty, goodness, and truth. Students determined to study what the world's great minds have said about the meaning of life have to turn to world religions courses, as I did, or sign up at sectarian religious schools.

Instead of holding educated convictions about God, death, love, morality, and beliefs that matter, Canadians have opted for a free-floating relativism, a kind of tolerant, easygoing spiritual "whatever." They're often curious about things related to divinity, and polls show that many have private experiences they consider transcendentally significant, but just don't expect to have an informed discussion with them on religion (which most link with institutions) or spirituality (the looser term many now associate with personal inner experiences).

Pope Benedict XVI was on to something in 2005, at least in part, when he attacked the western world's pervasive relativism, charging that it "does not recognize anything as absolute and leaves as ultimate only the measure of each one's ego and his desires." Although I don't agree with Benedict's utter denunciation of relativism, it is a concern that many Canadians seem to believe there is no such thing as truth, no basis for saying some things are more beautiful and authentic than others.

Pluralism is one of the reasons for this era's dearth of spiritual conviction and abundance of credulity. As Canada's greatest living philosopher, Charles Taylor, says in his 2007 book, *A Secular Age*, a few centuries ago it was almost impossible not to believe in God. Now it's just one option among many, says Taylor, who has Catholic roots, and being religious exposes one to stigmatization.

With no one religion dominating in Canada, except perhaps the civil "religion" of secularism, many people feel overwhelmed by all the isms that exist, from Buddhism to Judaism, libertarianism to consumerism, socialism to liberalism. They've become lost in a churning sea of world views; have come to think truth is just a matter of opinion.

And anyway, the rent has to be paid. Who has time for thinking seriously about such things?

How can we hold intelligent and strong spiritual convictions in a pluralistic world?

It's a question I face daily, as I write about the breathtaking—often inspiring, often disturbing—variety of religious belief and experience in Canada and around the planet.

However, part of the reason I keep enjoying my job, without being torn apart by the myriad religious and secular beliefs I write about, is that I hold to provisional convictions. These are ethical and spiritual truths that feel so thoroughly tested I no longer really doubt them. Although these truths often cannot be proven with empirical evidence, they can be intellectually defended, shown to be more logical and coherent than competing ideas.

Even though I was raised in a staunchly atheist family, I now feel strongly bolstered by neoclassical western philosophy (rooted in Plato and filtered through twentieth-century thinkers such as Alfred North Whitehead) and some streams of Christianity. For me, the life spirit—God—is not a dictatorial power but the persuasive entity that draws all living things toward creativity, goodness, and elegance. To me, Jesus, more than anyone we know, fully and bravely embodied God's sacred call to creative transformation.

In the evangelical world, my position would be closest to something called "open theism," as taught by Canadian theologians such as Clark Pinnock, who was at Vancouver's evangelical Regent College before moving to McMaster Divinity

College in Ontario. Open theism counters classic western theological traditions that hold up God as unchangeable, as having predetermined the future. It accepts free will as a reality. It envisions the future as unpredictable in some ways, even to God.

For me, Easter is a time when I celebrate how God ultimately overcomes the cruel, brute force that led to Jesus' crucifixion. God felt Jesus' suffering in the deepest, deepest way. The agony of Jesus, who incarnated or embodied the divine, made clear that a tender God was and is one with humanity, with all living things. The cross and resurrection reveal how God experiences the world's ecstasy and pain, while constantly persuading us, in every moment, to become co-creators in divine love.

In such an open-ended universe, surprise is possible—and the search for truth is eternal. Behaving as if one has forever nailed down the absolute truth suggests a lack of humility, I believe, a human assumption of divine omniscience. Being Christian doesn't mean acting as if the market's been cornered on The Answer or as if the institution one attends has captured it for all time. It means being open, as I think Jesus was, to trying to live out the truth wherever one, with the support of a mature spiritual community, discerns it.

My western-rooted Christian religious convictions, for instance, have been enhanced by studying the truths of Buddhism, which teaches liberation from pure self-interest, that everything in the universe is interdependent, that sometimes it's important to get beyond ideas and just experience life in its fullest. My willingness to refine my provisional truths encourages me to learn from scientists who teach that evolution is a process of both chance and purpose. I've appreciated the way Hindus talk about the four paths, or disciplines, to God: compassionate deeds (karma yoga), meditation (raja yoga), devotion (shakti yoga), and knowledge (jnana yoga).

Given my atheist upbringing and predilection to curiosity, I lean toward the path of knowledge. It's a route that suits a journalist.

I've also had the good fortune to learn a great deal about ultimate questions from the people I meet through my work. Two of the most beautiful human beings I've had the privilege to interview had profound convictions about the meaning of life: Catholic author and psychotherapist Henri Nouwen, and Canadian fiction writer Carol Shields.

Although Nouwen's Christianity may seem to be in conflict with Shields' professed atheism, these tender-hearted intellectuals, both of whom died in their sixties, held up as their ultimate truth the mysterious transforming reality of love. I still feel moved when I think about our personal, even intimate, encounters in the 1990s. Both turned into what the Jewish theologian, Martin Buber, called "I–thou" relationships.

"I think all my life I've felt close to God, particularly close to Jesus," Nouwen told me during an extensive conversation in which he took as much interest in my life as I in his. "On the other hand, I've had to rediscover Jesus over and over again. And one thing I have discovered is the spirit of Jesus blows where it wants ... I have this incredible feeling there are no boundaries and God loves everyone."

When I talked with Shields, who had been a United Church member and a Quaker, she claimed she no longer believed in God or, as she said, "a Mind behind the universe." But she talked passionately of the "sacred patterns" she found in each person's uniqueness.

Shields experienced moments when she touched the "transcendent." Of love she said: "I think it's the basic building block. It's your basic molecule." To her it linked all things. "Why else would we make an effort to be sort of good in the world and with one another, if it wasn't for this kind of mystical connection that holds us all together?" she asked. "Why else would we do it?"

Why indeed? As far as provisional beliefs go, I can affirm with Nouwen and Shields that there seems nothing more important in this difficult world than the transcendent, mysterious, unpredictable power of love. For me its source is the divine.

---

Although raised in a family of staunch atheists, Douglas Todd has gone on to become one of North America's most decorated spirituality and ethics writers. A columnist for the *Vancouver Sun*, he has twice won the Templeton Religion Reporter of the Year Award, the only Canadian to have received it. He is the author of several books, including the recent *Cascadia: The Elusive Utopia*, and *Brave Souls: Writers and Artists Wrestle with God, Love, Death and the Things That Matter*. He lives in Vancouver.

# On Monks, Monsters, and Manuscripts
~ *Michael W. Higgins* ~

I have been asked to reflect on the writing life, and since I am more familiar with my own life than any other, it seemed to me not altogether inappropriate to engage in a tantalizing mite of autobiography.

But first a cautionary tale.

Ian Hamilton's *New Yorker* article of February 28, 1994, on Stephen Spender has this to say of the eminent poet-critic's penchant for self-disclosure: "Throughout his career, he has given rise to several varieties of puzzlement. A saint or a schemer? A victim of fashion or a skilful self-advancer? A talent neglected or a small gift made too much of?"

I hope it will not be said of me what Hamilton astutely noted of the enigmatical and self-absorbed Spender, "that he has given us more than we can easily digest—a surfeit of self-exploration." I see myself in some ways as an intellectual and artistic dilettante, verily, a puzzlement: I was destined for the academy but I really prefer the stage. I was destined to write scripts about seminal spiritual figures, but I really want to be pope.

The Barbadian-Canadian novelist and short story writer Austin Clarke once observed, in his function as Visiting Professor of Creative Writing at Yale, that my writing, in contrast with that of the others in a creative writing seminar at St. Francis Xavier University in Nova Scotia, left him without comment. He was speechless. On another occasion a now-deceased editor of one of Atlantic Canada's leading literary journals, and himself a poet and critic, observed that my writing betrayed the voice of a singlety, a great something. You can see from these ambivalent accolades that I did not burst upon the literary scene. I suppurated.

I began with the theatre. First, there was *The Maccabean,* a play Professor Lambert of Ryerson in Toronto deemed

worthy of radical reinvention. And then there was *Besieged,* a
play set during the First Crusades, which if it had ever been
performed would have undermined the ecumenical goodwill
built up over the last half-century. Finally, there was *Rolfe:
A Mind Wondrous and Singular,* which enjoyed a run of two
performances. Not enough for off-Broadway, or anywhere
near Broadway for that matter, but at least it saw the light of
production. It was deemed by some critics an estimable farce.
It had, however, been conceived as a tragedy.

These are all perfect examples, nay flawless ones, of
closet drama. That's why the phrase "coming out of the closet"
generates such dread for me—the frightful possibility of having revealed in the full light of day my paltry theatrical offer-
ings. So my career as a dramatist came sputtering to an end.
Undaunted, I turned my attention to scripts. Or rather, more
precisely, I had it turned for me.

Now scriptwriters of whatever fashion are not particularly visible. We are often as acknowledged a species as ghostwriters, or more aptly, for those of us inclined to theological
and religious subjects, holy ghostwriters. In this regard I am
reminded of George S. Kaufman, who, having penned a script
for the Marx Brothers, paused on his way out of the theatre
following a rehearsal. "What's the matter, George?" inquired
one of his friends. "Oh, nothing," Kaufman replied smoothly,
"I just thought I heard one of my lines there for a moment."

Kaufman's experience with the Marx Brothers is akin to that
endured once by art and culture writer Gary Michael Dault while
working on the Sir Peter Ustinov *Inside the Vatican* series. As the
chief of the research team for the series, and as the script consultant for Dault, I can attest to the macabre and Byzantine intrigues
and tempests that accompanied working with Sir Peter and producer John McGreevy. Doctor Snuggles isn't always self-effacing.

It was in 1977 that my career as a scriptwriter, or documentarist as we are called in the "Corpse" (Canadian Broad-

casting Corporation), began. An Anglican priest-scholar and I were finishing our doctorates—in theology and English literature respectively—on the cloistered monk Thomas Merton, who disposed of himself by practical mishap in Bangkok.

A conference, organized with the support of the English and Religious Studies departments of the University of British Columbia and the Canada Council, was convened on the very shoulders of Wreck Beach—the nudist enclave—and drew scores of scholars, a scattering of monks, and a legion of libidinous onlookers. George Woodcock was there. Of course, George Woodcock was everywhere, but on this occasion he was present as the author of a new book, *Thomas Merton: Monk and Poet*. It was a sign of our boldness that my colleague and I prevailed on Mr. Woodcock to write a book on Merton for the princely sum of $1,500 which we had to borrow from my friend's father. (On a rather lugubrious note, we paid him back fifteen years later, on his deathbed.)

You can see that our temerity knew no bounds. And so one wintry day my colleague and I invited the executive producer of CBC's *Ideas*, Ms. Geraldine Sherman, for a drink to discuss our proposal for a series on Merton, the poet and thinker. She knew nothing of him. But she liked his photograph. She agreed. And she paid for the drinks.

And so it came about that in May of 1978, the Vancouver studios of the CBC were instructed to send technicians to record all the papers and readings at the conference. And they did so.

But it wasn't our conference. Concurrently on the UBC campus there was a conference on Bigfoot, the Sasquatch, the Abominable Snowman, and other like species. For three days the CBC crew recorded everything they could on monsters.

The monks were forgotten!

But not in Toronto. Ms. Sherman phoned in October, wondering about the status of the tapes. I was puzzled. The crew hadn't shown up, I told her with mounting anxiety, and we hadn't complained because, well, we had concluded that the proposal was perhaps a passing fancy. Our luck couldn't possibly hold, we faultily reasoned. We did have Woodcock—of course we owed him money—and we had the monks and the nudes, so losing the CBC somehow didn't seem too catastrophic.

Sherman was not amused. She terminated our conversation. Once she had determined the problem—the substitution of the Loch Ness Monster for a Cistercian poet—she phoned back, reminded me in forceful terms that we had an agreement, and gave me two months to write, edit, and narrate a five-hour series.

And that's how I became a scriptwriter.

Over the ensuing fifteen years I have written series on such thinkers as Simone Weil and Teilhard de Chardin as well as on various issues and topics, including four programs for that irascible and versatile genius John Reeves, on the Maritains (Jacques and Raissa), on the pastoral poets Margaret Avison and R.S. Thomas, on the Pascals (Jacqueline and Blaise), and on the splendid riches of silence … a topic on which I can speak with inexhaustible ignorance.

But the scripts I particularly treasure were my reconstructed debates. The first of these was *On Socialism, Sex and Salvation:* a debate between GKC and GBS—Gilbert Keith Chesterton and George Bernard Shaw. On the face of it, the two men were strikingly dissimilar. Shaw was a socialist, an evolutionist, a teetotaller, and an Irishman. Chesterton was a distributist—that is, he affirmed the principle of private property and believed that effective self-government required a truly distributed private property—a believer in orthodox religion, a debunker of modern myths, an imbiber, and an Englishman.

Shaw once referred to Chesterton as a man of colossal genius and infinite vest. Chesterton, in turn, accused Shaw of being a Puritan: "You will never admit of any of your jokes that it is only a joke. For instance, you ask people to worship the LIFE-FORCE; as if one could worship a hyphen."

My producer, Bernie Lucht, was firm of purpose in hunting down the actors appropriate for the roles. He lured Herb Foster from New York, where he was performing in his one-man show on G.B. Shaw; Tony Van Bridge from out West, where he was touring with his one-man show on G.K. Chesterton; and Lister Sinclair from Toronto, where he was performing in his one-man show on Lister Sinclair.

Librarians were invaluable in helping me scour the sources for vestiges of earlier debates, supplementing report-age and published transcripts with juicy chunks from letters, diaries, journalistic pieces, memoirs, and reminiscences. It was a formidable task, and out of a seemingly inchoate mass of materials I was able to sculpt a debate that never happened but should have. The script was performed before a live audi-ence—as if there could be any other kind—at Ignatieff The-atre, Trinity College, Toronto, was aired on several subsequent occasions, and even performed by a theatre group in New Brunswick.

I was riding high with this one. I even found myself mingling with the post-performance crowd, shyly noting that this line was mine, here I improved on a passage by GKC, there I deleted a solecism by Shaw, and could anyone quite ape Hilaire Belloc's baroque and pompous prose better than I (although this struck me later as a somewhat peculiar boast).

I was resolved this time that the scriptwriter would get noticed. Next time I would wish otherwise.

Following the success of *On Socialism, Sex and Salva-tion*—in which there had been a great deal of socialism, a little salvation, and no sex whatever—Bernie Lucht decided to best it with another reconstructed debate and this time with a debate that actually happened as recorded. And so, pumped

full of vainglory, I suggested the famous debate held at Oxford
in 1860 between Soapy Sam Wilberforce, the Lord Bishop
of Oxford, and Thomas Henry Huxley, Charles Darwin's
bulldog. It was my intention to recapture something of the
fervour, intellectual intensity, and moral earnestness of the
celebrated debate occasioned by Mr. Darwin's 1859 book: *On
the Origin of Species, by means of Natural Selection; or the Preserva-
tion of Favoured Races in the Struggle for Life*.

It appeared to me, on the surface, to be the least strenu-
ous assignment as a documentarist I had yet faced. I would
simply secure for myself the complete transcription of the
debate. After all, everyone knew the Bishop's famous thrust
and Huxley's equally celebrated parry:

> *Wilberforce:* I should like to ask Professor Huxley, who is
> sitting by me, and is about to tear me to pieces when I
> have sat down, as to his belief in being descended from
> an ape. Is it on his grandfather's or his grandmother's side
> that the ape ancestry comes in?

> *Huxley:* I assert—and I repeat—that a man has no rea-
> son to be ashamed of having an ape for his grandfather.
> If there were an ancestor whom I should feel shame in
> recalling it would rather be a man—a man of restless and
> versatile intellect—who, not content with an equivocal
> success in his own sphere of activity, plunges into scientif-
> ic questions with which he has no real acquaintance, only
> to obscure them by aimless rhetoric, and distract the at-
> tention of his hearers from the point at issue by eloquent
> digressions and skilled appeals to religious prejudice.

Poor Soapy!
Poor me! I soon discovered, with appropriate horror, that
no such complete transcription exists. In fact, there are compet-

ing versions of the exchange just quoted. I fell upon the librarians of St. Jerome's, Dana Porter at the University of Waterloo, as well as the Robarts Library in Toronto with abject and shameless abandon. With their assistance I searched frantically through every commentary and report of the debate that they could unearth for me; I combed through the many diary entries and correspondence allusions of Darwin's contemporaries—those to which I could gain access, that is—but there was very little, and what there was was deeply controverted.

It was not a matter of reconstructing a debate. It was a matter of inventing one.

And so, at our dress rehearsal, with the imposing Douglas Campbell as Wilberforce and the veteran stage actor Colin Fox as Huxley, we proceeded to re-enact the debate. It was lifeless. Lister Sinclair suggested incorporating Vice-Admiral Fitzroy, the captain of the *Beagle,* the ship upon which Darwin gathered his data for his natural selection hypothesis. A naturalist himself, a man of cultivated tastes and native curiosity, Fitzroy was also a devout Christian who never forgave himself for serving as an unwitting instrument for the advancement of Darwin's impious theory.

Like many good Victorians Fitzroy went mad, but not before I included him in the debate.

And so *On Fossils, Apes, and Angels* premiered at St. Jerome's University and shortly after aired on the national network. Fitzroy gave it some life—tortured life, but life nonetheless. But one problem remained. Fitzroy appeared not to have been there after all. Still, screen and stage actor Gillie Fenwick defossilized the debate, at least for a time, and dramatic licence once again had its day.

The travails of scriptwriting, for radio or TV, are many. Producers and hosts have their say, and they are not always sensitive to the cadences, balances, and felicities of language, or the facts of history.

But it has also been my experience that the producers of
CBC Radio programs are generally as fair as they are exacting,
informed as they are inquisitive. They are the most disinter-
ested crew one is likely to find anywhere. And they are also
savagely persistent taskmasters. While working on *Catholics,* an
*Ideas* series that I did in collaboration with producer Damiano
Pietropaolo, I was frequently sent scurrying for original
tape, riveting ambiance, the perfect test of a sound bite, the
captivating phrase uttered against a backdrop suggestive and
threatening. Writing the script was the easy part.

During the fine edit of "The Sign of the Crozier," the
second part of the series, Pietropaolo wanted to highlight
the dramatic contest of opposing ecclesiological and political
interests characteristic of the pontificate of John Paul II by setting the pope's formidable presence, with its prestige, power,
and pomp, against the stark, sane, and simple backdrop of
*campesino* rebellion. The pontiff and the priest; Pontifex Maximus
and the poet; John Paul and Ernesto Cardenal. And so, juxtaposed with the professionally recorded and firmly delivered
pontifical prose could be heard the roughly recorded and
hesitantly enunciated prophetical verse. It was a masterstroke,
with the dramatic impact reverberating throughout the rest of
the four-part series.

On another occasion, while working with Pietropaolo on
the series *Monasticism as Rebellion,* I learned the art of the bold
edit. Careful splicing and judicious interweaving of commentary, narrative, and music—the common tools of the trade—
can often give the impression of a finely wrought product: a
smooth, effortlessly realized intellectual and artistic construct.
The bold edit shatters this illusion by introducing the unpol-
ished, rustic edge of unadorned reportage into the disciplined
world of the perfect edit. A little Brecht never hurts.

What we did, in a manner reminiscent of the antiphonal
chanting of the psalms, was to alternate the lush and sensuous

cadences of Gregorian chant, as sung in a traditional convent of Benedictine nuns, with the often politicized but deeply spiritual insights of that exquisite U.S. rhetorician and Benedictine feminist, Sister Joan Chittister.

To get a series ready for airing—"in the can," as they say—requires a sturdy combination of energy, patience, creativity, cooperation, and sometimes mind-numbing pressure. The radio documentarist is a hybrid: technician, editor, and storyteller. A kind of writer who, I dare to believe, has a vital role to play in preventing what Timothy Findley calls "our civilization's falling away from articulation. On the one hand, the airy incoherence of televised lines—and on the other hand, the dense incoherence of academic criticism that has driven fiction to the wall."

In Canada, radio scripting has become a form of culture-saving, CBC Radio a mode of articulation, my mode, modest but assuming.

---

Michael W. Higgins is Professor of English and Religious Studies as well as President and Vice-Chancellor of St. Thomas University in Fredericton, New Brunswick. A native Torontonian, he is author and co-author of numerous books, including most recently *Stalking the Holy: In Pursuit of Saint-Making*; a documentarist for the CBC; papal affairs commentator for CTV; a columnist for *The Catholic Register*; and a regular contributor to the *Literary Review of Canada* and the *Globe and Mail*.

# Finding a Prophetic Perspective
~ *Bill Blaikie* ~

Engagement with both the church and the political process
is a feature of my life that goes back quite far. In 1960, at age
nine, I was well into many years of perfect attendance at Sunday school. I remember also eagerly watching the Nixon-
Kennedy debates on TV and being aware of discussions about
the possibility of a Catholic becoming president and whether
that would result in some inappropriate imposition of Kennedy's personal religion on his political decisions.

I was brought up a Christian in the context of Transcona
Memorial United Church, in the working-class Winnipeg
suburb of Transcona. Most men there worked for the Canadian National Railway. My father, Bob Blaikie, was a machinist
by trade. Indeed, one didn't usually inquire who your father
worked for, but rather what he did at CN. The CN Shops in
Transcona were publicly owned then and employed thousands.
(Today there are fewer than 500 workers, and thanks to a
privatized merger with Illinois Central, CN is an open sore
through which the virus of an entirely different and nastier
labour-management culture is establishing itself in this
country. But that is a story for another day, a story of national
betrayal and shame that has gone largely untold.)

I grew up in that church, surrounded (as I later realized)
by many CCF-NDP voters, without being conscious of the
social gospel tradition, the connection between Christian
activism and politics in Canada, J.S. Woodsworth, or the Rev.
Stanley Knowles. This might have been, in part, because feder-
ally Transcona belonged to the St. Boniface riding at the time
and so we didn't have the instructive opportunity of a federal
incumbent like Stanley Knowles, as our neighbours in Winnipeg's North End did. But most of all, I think, I was unaware
of the political dimension of the gospel because I was brought
up in a Christian world view that was apolitical, or at least saw

itself as apolitical, although of course that apparent apolitical quality was in fact an incredibly political way of communicating the gospel.

In the meantime, I was absorbing the biblical tradition, getting to know the foundational stories of Judeo-Christian civilization, and learning hymns and children's songs that still stand me in good stead in difficult times. I would wager that all those United Church men and women who over the years ran for the NDP in hopeless ridings went to their political doom humming "Dare to Be a Daniel," as opposed to reciting some particular theological argument for democratic socialism.

By the time I got to the University of Winnipeg in 1969, I was part of a generation that was questioning the notion that we were obliged to uncritically accept whatever was being done by the United States or others in the name of containing communism, much as we are now expected to accept whatever is done in the name of security or fighting terrorism. My first inkling, actually, that something was wrong was in October 1962 during the Cuban Missile Crisis, when I thought the world was going to end. That experience made me a lifelong opponent of nuclear weapons and an advocate of nuclear disarmament, a Christian position if there ever was one.

Later, the war in Vietnam would become an occasion for mass prophetic consciousness creation. The prophetic perspective is one that dares to imagine one's own side might be wrong, might be sinful, might be motivated by something other than what official propaganda tells us is the case. This didn't always come easy to a generation steeped in the righteousness of the Allied cause in World War II (a righteousness I do not question). It wasn't easy for the generation that fought World War II to have its children be cynical about the moral integrity of the world they had fought to create. But no one, least of all the prophets, ever said being prophetic is a pleasant or an easy business. It has to be done with love rather than loathing and in a way that appeals to the best of a people's tradition rather than calling on them to abandon their traditions, but even then it is seldom welcome. Nor does all political protest or criticism pass this test.

I hadn't encountered the prophetic tradition in my United Church upbringing. There wasn't a lot of "Christ *against* Culture," to use H. Richard Niebuhr's typology, more the "Christ *of* Culture," unless you were talking cultures of sinful personal behaviour like drinking, sexual infidelity, swearing, gambling, etc., or personal dishonest behaviours like lying and stealing. It was an ethic limited to the personal behaviour of individuals, not extended to the political and economic behaviour of institutions, those powerful enough to run them, or those with the potential in a democratic society—voters, that is—to change corporate behaviour or challenge the power of the powerful. I didn't yet realize that, as someone once observed, the Canadian Left owed as much to Methodism as it did to Marx.

I would have to wait to learn that salvation might mean being saved not only from destructive personal behaviour, but from destructive and dangerous workplaces, oppressive relationships, and economic injustice. Issues like abortion and capital punishment aren't the only moral issues. The economy is a moral issue, and more and more research on the teachings of Jesus points to the original economic meaning of many of his parables, as well as to the original political significance of confessing Jesus as Lord in an imperial context that used the same language to describe the emperor.

It was a non-prophetic Christianity I was questioning when I took a course in Religious Studies from Charles Newcombe, who had been professor of Old Testament at United College (now University of Winnipeg) for many years. I had enrolled for a course called Literature of the Bible, taught by Carl Ridd, who would become an important teacher and

friend. But that very popular course was full—and I have never regretted that it was. Charlie Newcombe taught his class
the politics of the biblical stories. He made us see that the
prophets were critical of kings and kingdoms on the basis of
how they were treating their people, whether the vulnerable
were being looked after, whether justice was being done. God
was concerned about what was going on outside the temple
and not necessarily impressed with what went on inside it.
I learned that God takes sides. It stirred in me a hope that I
could find a way of bringing biblical faith and the real world I
was experiencing into some kind of helpful dialogue.

Later at the University of Winnipeg, another teacher,
mentor, and friend, John Badertscher, invited William Stringfellow to speak. Stringfellow was active with the Berrigan
brothers in opposing the draft in the United States and wrote
a book entitled *An Ethic for Christians and Other Aliens in a
Strange Land*. The book described America as Babylon, in the
biblical sense, and talked about Christians as exiles. I em-
braced this way of thinking at one level, but was in tension
with it at another.

Just before that particular year I had watched the 1971
New Democratic Party leadership convention on TV. Listening to speeches from the likes of Tommy Douglas, M.J.
Caldwell, and David Lewis, I had been converted to the idea
of politics as transformative rather than as a form of resistance
or protest, or for that matter, a clash of interests as it is usually
rendered by small-*l* liberal analysis. I had glimpsed in the NDP
the presence of a prophetic politics. Here was a political party
not unwilling to challenge the powerful or to be critical of
popular positions or prejudices.

I remember a discussion I had some years later with Phil
Berrigan, who visited a house church community I was part
of at Emmanuel College. Phil was convinced of the futility of
conventional—that is, electoral—politics. I didn't agree with

him, and I still don't, although there are days I wonder. I also
wonder whether the differences between us were ultimately
theological, or whether in part they reflected differences between the Canadian and American context. Policies, positions,
and perspectives that are hard to find in the U.S. Congress,
even on an individual basis, are often represented in the Canadian Parliament by a party that actually gets elected, albeit in
small numbers.

And Canada itself is not Babylon. Canada may be a vassal
state but it does have a different social and economic ethos
(although it's eroding), and it sometimes abstains from things
like the invasion of Iraq or Ballistic Missile Defense, even if it
can't bring itself to criticize what it won't participate in. And
if the free market is the false god, the idol we are all being
compelled to worship courtesy of free-market fundamentalism, then Canada has had anti-Babylonian features we should
cherish and defend. We have not done all things—in culture,
broadcasting, health care, generic drugs, wheat marketing,
supply management, transportation, post-secondary education—by the free market. But the NAFTA (North American
Free Trade Agreement) and the WTO (World Trade Organization) are designed to eliminate these distinctions, and the
process, already well begun, continues.

Phil Berrigan spent the last few years of his life in prison.
I wrote him just before his death a few years ago to remind
him of our conversation and to let him know what I'd been
up to. He was kind enough not to suggest, in reply, that I had
been wasting my time.

When I graduated from the Toronto School of Theology
in 1977 it was at the height of the debate about the Mackenzie
Valley Pipeline. Ecumenical justice coalitions abounded and
a new critique of our way of life was being developed out of
opposition to our uncritical habits of energy consumption and
all that was involved in securing new sources of that energy,

particularly in the North. It seemed at that time, just before the Reagan-Mulroney era of deregulation and privatization put off facing ecological realities for a generation, that we were on the brink of really doing something different. It turns out we weren't, but we will be some day, because we're running out of oil and the sooner we get busy on the alternatives the better.

In 1974 I had begun three years of study at the Toronto School of Theology. I went on a fellowship designed for those who were thinking of ministry but still undecided. It was a life-changing experience. Among other things, I heard a great sermon by Dr. Greer Boyce based on Matthew 10:34, where Jesus says he came not to bring peace but rather a sword. This was important to me, as I was having a hard time reconciling the divisive and demanding nature of Christ's teachings with the culture of being nice and pastoral I associated with being a good Christian. The idea that being faithful might in some circumstances also involve confrontation gave me permission to more seriously consider seeking ordination, which I did.

While in Toronto, I was exposed to liberation theology at St. Michael's College. More importantly, my knowledge of the social gospel and the interaction between religion and politics was deepened through many informal conversations I was privileged to have with Roger Hutchinson and Gregory Baum. At that time Hutchinson was a professor of Religious Studies at Victoria University in Toronto and Baum was at the Institute for Christian Thought. Hutchinson would later become principal of Emmanuel College and Baum is now professor emeritus at McGill. I was also influenced by the work I did with Dr. Ernie Best, my supervisor in a directed individual study on Frederick Denison Maurice, a prominent nineteenth-century Christian socialist in England.

I remember Gregory Baum saying something to the effect that what divided Christians was no longer denominational, but rather their attitude toward Christendom and its demise. The real division, that is, was between those who welcomed Christendom's demise as an opportunity for a more authentic Christian life and those who lamented the demise and sought to resist it. This is perhaps even truer today than it was then, as the post-Christendom reality sinks in.

I believe that understanding the post-Christendom context, and subsequently, how to live faithfully in it, is the central challenge for all of us who confess Jesus as Lord. What does it mean to say that Jesus is Lord in this context?

I think I know what it means for me, or should. If Jesus is Lord, then the market isn't. If Jesus is Lord, then my own prejudices and interests aren't. If Jesus is Lord, then even the superpowers must answer to his teachings. If Jesus is Lord, then he is Lord of all creation, and all creation is the object of God's love. For God so loved the world— not individuals, but the world—that he gave his only begotten Son.

But what does it mean to others when they hear someone say Jesus is Lord? How do we employ religious language in public discourse in a way that doesn't offend, or at least not in an inappropriate way? There is an appropriate offense to the gospel. But the inappropriate offense in the post-Christendom world is, I believe, sounding like you want to re-establish Christendom. It may also be inappropriate to be hostile to the reality of a multifaith, multicultural, secular, pluralistic society, but not inappropriate to ask constructive, even difficult, questions about how such a reality is to be understood and managed.

It seems to me there is an even greater level of challenge in figuring out how to practise a prophetic Christian faith in the post-Christendom context. Sometimes I feel that even though many of us understand we're in this context, our prophetic perspective sounds as if we're calling post-Christendom to act justly in the same way we might have called Christendom to act. We are not like the Hebrew prophets who could speak out of and into a tradition to which all felt accountable. We are not like an Archbishop William Temple or a Frederick Denison Maurice in nineteenth-century England, or the Fellowship for a Christian Social Order in the 1930s here in Canada.

How do we clothe the naked public square Richard John Neuhaus spoke about in his book by the same name, without being open to the charge of being theocrats? Incidentally, Mr. Neuhaus doesn't mind leaving the marketplace naked when it comes to religion and values, and I think this is a fatal flaw in his theology. On the other hand, Canadian theologian Douglas John Hall has done some good work on setting out a confessional model of how to speak about our faith, as opposed to an exclusivist or for that matter uncritically inclusivist approach in which all distinctive meaning is lost.

I agree with Jim Wallis of the Sojourners community in Washington DC, when he says not only that the Right gets it wrong, but that the Left doesn't get it. Both he and Rabbi Michael Lerner, author of *The Left Hand of God*, have done a great service to American politics by arguing that the Left and the Right each need to be challenged by faith in their own way, and that the Left needs to recover and reclaim its religious roots. There is a similar but not identical need in Canadian politics, a need recognized by the NDP in 2006 when the Faith and Social Justice caucus was formally set up to acknowledge the continuing reality of Canadians coming to their left-wing politics out of religious conviction.

It has become increasingly important to me in recent years to challenge the monopoly, or copyright, that elements of the so-called Christian Right have on the image of Christianity in the public domain. Christians or other religious people involved in progressive politics need to be more up front and less timid about where they are coming from. If the Christian Right gets to represent religion in the political discourse, it becomes a stumbling block to many on the progressive side of the political spectrum who might otherwise be more open to, benefit from, and be challenged by seeing the relationship between their values and biblical teachings. Further, this monopoly provokes a reactive secular fundamentalism that is not good. This stereotyping of religion is also a problem for many in the more conservative and/or evangelical Christian community, where a diversity of opinion on many things is missed in such stereotyping.

In any event, Christians who don't normally agree with each other must continue to maintain that the public square is a place for religious language and argument, properly offered by Christians who see that faith and politics go together, faith informing politics and politics contextualizing faith. The hope is that this kind of defensive ecumenical endeavour might yet lead to newer forms of unity. As the culture wars either end or come to be handled differently, and as issues like poverty, inequality, and protecting and preserving creation become more and more salient, I cherish the hope that Christians across the political spectrum will yet be inspired to work together.

------

Hon. Bill Blaikie, M.P., a minister of the United Church of Canada, has represented Winnipeg's Elmwood-Transcona federal riding in the Canadian Parliament since 1979, serving numerous critic roles for the New Democratic Party (NDP), culminating in service as NDP House Leader and Parliamentary Leader. In April 2006 he was appointed Deputy Speaker of the House. In 2007 he was awarded Parliamentarian of the Year by his peers. He has been appointed adjunct professor of Theology and Politics at the University of Winnipeg in anticipation of the end of the Thirty-Ninth Parliament when, not seeking re-election, he intends to spend more time reflecting and writing about the relationship between faith and politics.

# El Marahka IV[1]

~ *Trevor Herriot* ~

"Who is fit to climb God's mountain / and stand in his holy place?" the shepherd-king asked. It is tempting to try to sneak back up along the old pathways. Some have tried it in their hearts, to return to that pre-literate age of magic and myth, to the time before the written word usurped the shaman's power. Halfway to the top they decided that was far enough and set up camp. First thing they did was get a printing press and start publishing newsletters and books for the aspiring pagan. And that was where it ended: with one mystery appropriating another.

David's answer? "Whoever has integrity: / not chasing shadows, / not living lies." The neo-pagan shortcut is fraught with shadows because we let the genie out of the bottle three thousand years ago. Once a powerful tool, the alphabet, is harnessed to a powerful idea, monotheism, the resulting Word unleashed upon the world leaves us wounded and exiled. If we are unfit to make the climb, it is because we are hobbled by the same exile and desire that made the Israelites dance in obeisance to two gods. "How long," asked Elijah, "do you mean to hobble first on one leg then on the other?" The Israelites had no reply for that question and I wonder if we are any nearer an answer today.

&#x0253;

A Christian by birth, culture, and upbringing, like many of my time I have had my lapses and relapses away from and back toward the Church, in my case Roman Catholicism. There is no shortage of justification for leaving the Church—its

---

1    Psalm 24:3; translation from Hebrew into English poetry, from the English translation of *The Liturgical Psalter* (International Committee on English in the Liturgy, Inc., 1994).

culpability in the conquest of the New World and the oppression of its peoples, an entrenched fear of women, a record of attracting and hiding sexually deviant priests, pewfuls of self-serving and smug parishioners, corrupt and dogmatic hierarchy, lifeless liturgies, and so on. All fine and virtuous reasons to proudly join the ranks of former Catholics, but the last time I shook the dust of Catholicism from my feet, leading the way up onto the moral high road was my ego, freshly wounded in a personal encounter with ecclesial cowardice.

Karen and I were young enough to know everything then. That the premier's wife and another one of the most influential Catholics in the diocese—both major donors in the Church's recent fundraising campaign—had been in for tea with the archbishop before he called us in. That we were right and they were wrong. That the missives we'd written in the social justice newsletter, aimed at the province's Conservative government, had made their mark. That the archbishop had promised them the political attacks would stop. And that now, after our chastening and a final pudgy-fingered blessing—go and sin no more—we'd stride righteously away from his office, away from the Church that had finally proven itself beneath our virtue.

We'd long ago lost our tolerance for all that was retrograde in Catholicism: all that was decaying, backward-looking, afraid of women and other sources of change and renewal. We'd lost our patience, our hope for transformation, and our place in the Church, but we would find something else. We were happy to go and knew that somewhere outside the Church we'd locate that exemplary community of spiritual seekers who are all secure enough in their faith to honour the wilderness in God, to celebrate the unruly and protect the innocent, and to ignite the fires that unite us in mercy, pity, peace, and love.

During those five years away from Catholicism, though, I learned that life rages on with all of its corruption, loss, and disappointment regardless of where one stands in relation to church walls. The nonpareil circle of worship never materialized. Friends and relatives got sick. Beloved ones died: one of sorrow, many of age and disease. Governments continued their obsession with free trade, national security, and limitless growth. Farms continued to look more and more like firms, and rural people moved away to find jobs in distant cities where they bumped up against aboriginal people fleeing overcrowded and impoverished reserves.

Birds disappeared. Each spring I counted migrant songbirds in the mornings and tried vainly to convince myself that the numbers were not declining. Maybe it was just another overflight, or a natural dip in a long, sine-wave trend. Next spring, it won't be quite so bad. Sure, tropical deforestation, fragmentation of our boreal woodlands, and pesticide use are reducing the forest bird populations but maybe things aren't as hopeless as we think. The loss of local breeding prairie species was even harder to wish away. It took just three years for the small pastures near the city to give up their last few burrowing owls, chestnut-collared longspurs, Sprague's pipits, and Baird's sparrows.

I think I got weary of things going away, of sudden absences, until I was blind to small renewals, life hatching forth surprisingly as it does—not perfectly or on the terms of yesterday, but in new and surprising ways. I go to church now for the same reasons I have taken to walking a woebegone strip of native grass that runs along the railway tracks where they leave the city. Last time I went, I found a killdeer nest—four pointy-ended eggs, turned inward and nestled in a perfect little mandala. To get there, I walk west out of the city on a street that crosses the creek, turns to gravel, and leads past ball diamonds, a golf course, a nursery, and the RCMP grounds before things quiet down. If I keep up a good pace it takes me fifteen minutes from my doorstep to reach the first

meadowlark song. All along the walk I am a stone's throw
from the main CPR line, the one that laid steel upon the
dreams of the Eastern capital in the 1880s, the one that Chief
Piapot failed to stop with his teepee roadblock, the one that,
on a summer afternoon in 1882, bore a private train, with
CPR founder Sir Cornelius Van Horne and a gaggle of local
dignitaries aboard, to the creek crossing where they stopped
long enough to drink a toast and name the town in honour of
a dowager queen who would never see these plains. We live
a block from the line and at night when the freights go by
slowly I wake to the rattle of doorknobs and the low rumble
of fifteen thousand tons of God-knows-what-all rolling east or
west. Our children count boxcars from their bedroom windows and there is a sign at the end of our street commemorat-
ing the two thousand relief-camp refugees who jumped off the
train right there in June 1935 only to be bludgeoned, shot at,
and chased out of town by the RCMP on Canada Day three
weeks later.

The railway and its grassy easement are a blessing, a curse,
and the reason I am drawn to this path out of the city. It makes
for a mournful walk, a transect raw with the fresh wounds of
our encampment here on the Qu'Appelle plains. I see fewer
birds, fewer butterflies, fewer frogs every time I go but I keep
going. Between the gravel road and the rail bed, there runs a
strip of unmowed grass, weeds, and ditch-puddles—a scrap of
uncultivated land that ranges from seventy-five to two hundred
feet wide. Much of it is littered with old tires, drink cans, and
rotting lumber; almost all of it matted down with brome grass,
crested wheat grass, thistles, absinthe, and other introduced
species. It is an unkempt, shaggy place. Joggers and dog walkers
stay away in droves. Hidden in the weeds and still within the
western limits of the city, a vestige of native grass and forbs
runs here and there in discontinuous patches along the railway
easement. I can span the narrowest pieces with my outstretched

arms. Other places it may be twenty or thirty feet wide. With cropland on one side and the railroad and city on the other, this remnant of the old buffalo prairie is several miles away from any other. Aggressive weeds from other continents are encroaching on each patch, mingling with native grasses, three-flowered avens, asters, cinquefoil, and sage. There is not much good to be said for these Eurasian weeds, though they green up quickly in spring, keep the soil in place, and provide richer habitat than a wheat field.

Whenever I am out walking the easement, questions arise about the mix and unfolding of life there. Each step intersects points in time and space where the prairie remnant is changing and becoming something different here and now beyond human will, somewhere within the mysteries of Divine will. I flush two game birds from the snowberry in front of me and it is a thrill until I realize they are grey partridge, another introduced species. But I *like* grey partridge. From the standpoint of ecology, non-native is always bad and native is always good. Ideally there would be no mixing. In thrall to the lesser gods of science, I can't escape the coin-toss view of life as good or bad, true or untrue, native or alien. Walking the remnant, I catch myself cursing the untrue, the bad, and the alien, lamenting all that is gone, all that seems to be going: the prairie I knew as a boy, its birds, its self-reliant people and their stories, and its innocence, or at least my belief in its innocence. I stand in the midst of a landscape made by our transgressions and then something always surprises me. A circle of avens blooming on the ground as perfect in its green and red as an advent wreath. A mat of moss phlox silver and white covering a patch of ground the size of our front garden. Once, I watched a female Brewer's blackbird transform her drab brown cowl into her secret beauty—a veil of shimmering turquoise beadwork that hovers just above the surface of her back and wings to be seen only by her mate when the sun is just so.

Walking back into town on Sunday mornings I have heard the bells pealing from the towers of the cathedral. Holy Rosary is a mile and a half back along the avenue and when I look up at the city's skyline, the twin spires gleam above elms and rooftops. All of my children were baptized there with water that ran over their heads through the font basin and down to the cold clay beneath the nave of the church. Once, on a May afternoon I spoke sacred vows to their mother as we stood together beneath its vaulted ceilings facing a church full of family and friends. And on Sunday mornings now I stand shoulder to shoulder there with people whose theology and politics I may not like. Even so, we face our sins together, begging communal forgiveness and embracing communal hope in the reconciliation of irreconcilables, in belief in the unbelievable, in the life gestating within all that seems to be dying.

I am not sure what it is that keeps me returning to a prairie remnant and to church, but it feels the same. I stand within and bear witness to weeds, garbage, railway, and a few scattered wild things, all in one place, pay homage to the lives that are passing there, as my own is, as all lives are, face our trespasses with courage, ask for forgiveness, and dwell in the light as dim as it is amid the darkness. Now and then, there is a paschal moment when the hidden beauty of a blackbird shines forth on a spring morning, reminding me of regenerative powers that wait beneath and within.

When I went back to the cathedral again a few years ago I saw the unity in our ragtag diversity for the first time. The God who spun off 350,000 different beetles wouldn't be impressed by a homogenous battalion of worshippers anyway, no matter how virtuous or wise. So, here we are then, all in it together. Some looking for comfort amidst privilege and probity. Others hoping to shore up a flagging faith. Some seeking a private encounter with the Divine. Others seeking to merge with a body of believers. Some hoping to dissolve the pain of reality in the waters of heaven's promise. Others hoping to chasten themselves by facing the truth of our brokenness. Some nursing their piety with novenas while they cling to a mildewed dogma. Others holding fast to the prospects for religious renewal offered in new theology.

Despite all that divides us, we share in a struggle to believe the good news in a world where bad news is abundant and always easier to believe. Hammered by the believable lies that justify billion-dollar assaults in the Middle East, pesticides that support our "feed-the-world" mania, and technology that promises to help anyone have a baby and everyone live longer, we gather to the clanging of bells and try to see the truth in the body we form, in the Divinity who is a parent, a child, and a spirit all at once, in the standing up of the dead, and in the regaining of the lost.

Lost sheep, lost treasures, lost sons—this religion is so much about losing one's way or losing the richness of life, longing for it, and then regaining it amidst great feasting and celebration. If we've lost our way on the Mountain of the Lord, on our ascent from pagan hunter to post-Enlightenment Christian, how else to regain the path than to backtrack to the place where we veered away from God's own wildness? People can try to jump back along the journey to the rites of distant ancestors, but it makes more sense to start where the spoor is still fresh, where you can share sacraments in a living body of bodies who still believe in the possibility of transformation. What better place to reckon the sins of our civilization than here, in the church that once sang hosannas upon its reckless advance?

In solidarity with the spiritually unfit everywhere, I am making my way back to El Marahka to stand with the Israelites. There we will wait for Elijah to come along, disembowel the bull, toss it on the pyre, douse it with water, and call upon God's fire.

---

Trevor Herriot is a Regina writer and naturalist. He is the author of *River in a Dry Land: A Prairie Passage*, which won the Writer's Trust Drainie-Taylor Biography Prize and was shortlisted for a Governor's General Literary Award. His second book, *Jacob's Wound: A Search for the Spirit of Wildness*, was shortlisted for the Writer's Trust Award for Non-Fiction. His third book, *Grass, Sky, Song: The Gift of Grassland Birds*, will be published by HarperCollins in the spring of 2009.

# The Making of a Prairie Preacher
~ *Brian C. Stiller* ~

I was proud to be a preacher's kid in our Pentecostal church community in Saskatoon. When asked, "Are you Hilmer's son?" I answered with a strong "Yes." While our church was regarded as outside the mainstream, school friends and neighbours didn't seem to think the term "holy rollers" applied to us. We entered into life at school and found Saskatoon a place to call our own.

Dad was a son of the prairies, born into a Swedish Mission Covenant Church in Manitoba. In his early ministry, he and his brother Henning came in contact with Pentecostals and soon joined their ranks. Though he was a pastor, Dad didn't have a church; he superintended the fifty or so churches scattered across Saskatchewan. Whether he was home or not, Elim Tabernacle was the gravitational centre of our family's weekly life. Sunday included Sunday school and morning and evening services. Friday night was youth service. Regular evangelistic meetings ran for a week at a time, and many a night the Stiller family was there.

Pastors were poor, so when they came to visit their "bishop" they ate at our table and slept in our beds. They were family. Mom and Dad allowed us to sit and listen to their stories and heartaches. We watched as our parents lovingly took their broken and bruised lives, massaged their sore muscles, built back their spirits, told them of their importance, and then sent them on their way back to the small churches, hoping they could find significance and service in the harsh soil of their communities.

In the 1940s and '50s, a heresy stirred in the Pentecostal ranks, crushing many a congregation. "Latter Rain" was its name, a term gleaned from the Old Testament prophet Joel. It mixed a strong and simple faith with naïveté and religious hyperventilation. To use D.G. Hart's phrase, it was a "spiritual greenhouse." The bizarre behaviour and biblical exegesis of the splinter group made mainstream Pentecostals seem downright irenic. The epicentre of this movement was in the newly built Saskatoon Bethel Bible Institute.

By 1947, the division had become so contentious that Reverends George Hawtin and P.G. Hunt, both teachers at the school, moved to a new enterprise called Sharon Orphanage and Schools in North Battleford. A year later Dad was elected denominational head of the province. After some fifteen years serving Saskatchewan congregations, church leaders saw him as the kind of person they needed to lead in the turmoil.

Dad took up the task of bringing healing to a theologically divided and emotionally hurting community. Having survived the demands of the Depression, the abuse of the drought, and the patronizing glances and snide remarks of fellow church leaders, would this sectarian, Bible-thumping, tongues-speaking group survive?

An evangelist was "holding meetings" at a downtown Saskatoon hotel, hosted by a local independent minister. I was in my mid-teens and interested in learning for myself whether the report was indeed true that when the evangelist was "Spirit-anointed" oil would appear on his hands. Neither the summer exhibition nor the winter carnival could match such claims. It was time to check it out. So my friend and I decided to attend. However, when I heard the evangelist include my father in his list of those who were "servants of the devil," I got angry.

The local minister knew whose son I was. (I had tried earlier—without success—to date his daughter.) Seeing my agitation, he asked the evangelist to step aside and told the audience, "Bow your heads." He then proceeded to recount the Old Testament story of a group of teenagers who were killed by a bear when they ridiculed the prophet Elisha. He continued: "A young man made fun of my preaching and died within a few days." With that warning he pronounced that my friend and I would die within a week.

My friend and I were considered celebrities, at least until we lived past the prophesied day of doom. Dad, however, saw it as his issue. I was to leave my father's battles to him, not shoulder them myself. For a decade and a half, Dad steered this little denomination down a new track of thoughtful ministry, seeking to build a community that found its place within the wider community of faith.

There is a question I wish Dad were alive to answer. Each Christmas Eve, he encouraged us as teenagers to attend Catholic Mass. Remember, this was the 1950s in the rural world of the Midwest, and we were Pentecostal to boot. Our eschatology, wrapped up in dispensationalism, viewed Rome as the "Mother of Harlots." So why did Dad see going to Mass as not only permissible but valuable? I suspect he viewed the wider church of Jesus Christ as important. As odd and troubling as the variant theologies of "liberal" or Roman churches might have been to us, he knew our little church had grasped only a part of truth. He wanted his children to see the wider agenda and workings of the Spirit.

It was in this world that my desire and will to serve in the wider church found its beginning. One night, as Mom and Dad were about to turn out the lights, I walked into their bedroom and said, "I've decided to go to Bible college." They had never asked me about my future, but assumed I would soon choose.

That decision came out of years living in the shadow of my father. Three memories linger. The first is of Living Waters Camp. Built on Manitou Lake, near Watrous, it was a lake with high salt content and a specific gravity of 1.06 that makes one buoyant, much like the Dead Sea does. I suppose only Pentecostals had the optimism to construct a camp by the lake with such a high mineral content and call it "Living Waters." Aboriginal people called it the "Lake of Healing Waters" because of its curative powers.

Promptly after school was out in late June, I'd take the train to get an early jump on fixing up camp with Dad, along with many of his pastors, a few weeks before it opened. Dad was the cook, and for his "boys" he spared no expense for the best of daily fare. We loved to hear the stories, laugh at the jokes, and feel the loving banter as they worked together.

Then camp came. I looked forward to this gathering— friends from across the province, missionaries with stories and films, and preachers by the dozen. It was the only place to be, for there I could hear at least three sermons a day. I loved the power of the words. The stories of God's grace lifted Bible stories off the page. Dad was careful in whom he invited to preach; Pentecostals had their fair collection of carnival barkers. Prairie folk at the time had little besides the radio to instill a discerning mind, but they knew Dad's choices of preachers could be trusted.

One evening, the power of the message and presence of the speaker left me deeply moved. I went out behind the Tabernacle—with its wood shavings—and said yes to the Lord. That night Brother Spence had spoken. A missionary to China, he had been interned by the Japanese during the war. Now in his eighties and walking with a cane, that night he sang:

When I've gone the last mile of the way,
I will rest at the close of the day.
I know there are joys that await me
When I've gone the last mile of the way.

Then he announced he was returning to China. My prayer behind the Tabernacle was, "Lord if you are calling this old man, then the least I can do is to give you my life."

A second memory comes from my travels with Dad on his Sunday church visits. We'd head off early Sunday morning, down gravel roads, across current-driven ferries into towns where congregations would be waiting to hear "Brother Stiller." These Sundays were often special days; Thanksgiving, church anniversaries, or dedications. In Mennonite or Ukrainian communities, the church lunch afterwards was enough to hold the attention of any teenage boy worth his salt: perogies, *hulubtsi*, smoked sausage, *kovbasa*, chicken cooked in a thousand ways, salads of all kinds, and desserts of unbelievable goodness.

It was there that I listened to Dad speak in sermons. This was more than words; it was a distinct expectation that we would hear from the Lord. I watched Dad as he brought people to a moment of faith. They were there to touch "the hem of the Lord's garment."

In our small and socially marginalized prairie churches, nothing was as important as the sermon. We came to church to meet with and hear from God. We didn't argue over whether the Bible was true or not, we simply believed it was. More importantly, we wanted to know what it said. Not surprisingly, the sermon occupied the most important time of the service. In time I wanted to preach more than anything else.

I learned preaching not just from our denominational pastors and evangelists, but from our wider evangelical world. Youth for Christ spread its presence in the late 1940s. As I child I went with my mom and siblings to the Saskatoon Arena on Twenty-second Street to hear Charles Templeton, the Canadian who, like his counterpart Billy Graham in the United States, founded a national YFC movement. Every second Saturday night, at the YFC rallies in the Apostolic church at Nineteenth Street and Avenue G, we heard more preaching. Our family ritual on Sunday morning included the radio broadcasts of Charles E. Fuller's "Old Fashioned Revival Hour" from Long Beach, California, and Alberta premier E.C. Manning in "The Back to God Hour" from a theatre in downtown Edmonton.

My irrevocable call to the ministry came when I least expected it. It was the last spring of high school, and time to decide—would I follow my older brother Cal into university? Dad was home that weekend, and we were hosts to a missionary couple, Henry and Florence Koopman.

Years earlier, Henry Koopman had been attracted to missions in Africa, but our denominational mission board had decided he didn't have what it took and so turned him down. Determined, he sold his small farm in Asquith and bought a one-way ticket to West Africa, arriving with no mission agency as sponsor and no one to meet him. Some years later, he met Florence Fleming in Africa and they were married.

That morning when he preached, I was less than impressed. His antique double-breasted suit didn't pass the scrutiny of a seventeen-year-old who worked in Caswell's Men's Wear, which sold the finest haberdashery in the city.

Later, as we concluded our traditional Sunday dinner, Dad said, "Brian, I want you to take Brother and Sister Koopman to their various appointments and then bring them to church tonight." I choked; my plans were to hang out with friends, not escort primitive missionaries. But there it was: I was more told than asked. At least I had Dad's car for the afternoon.

After the Sunday night evangelistic service, I drove the Koopmans north on Avenue A to Bethel Bible Institute. Partway there, Brother Koopman asked, "Brian, drop me off here and take Sister Koopman to the school." After leaving her at the school, I circled around to see what this was all about. Parking back in the shadows, I saw this missionary—one who in his early days was not seen to be of missionary value for our church, but now one of its career missionaries—talking to an inebriated man leaning against a telephone pole. He had seen him on our drive and had chosen to complete the day with ministry to someone I hadn't even seen.

I sat and watched. I could see them in conversation, wondering how the man understood Henry Koopman's strong Dutch accent. But words may not have mattered. Eventually the missionary pulled out his wallet, slipped some money into the man's hand and left. I waited as he walked north. Then turning the corner to return home, I knew why I was there. I was brought face to face with my own smallness. While his preaching skills were not to my liking, I now had seen deeper into what mattered. I had been soundly rebuked by my superficial analysis and inflated sense of calling.

I sat outside our two-storey white house with black trim on 816 Rusholme Road, caught between the competing dynamics of self-interest and authenticity. "If this man could serve in Africa," I finally reasoned, "then the least I can do is prepare for ministry, wherever it may lead."

That night I went into my parent's bedroom and announced, "Mom, Dad, I'm applying to go to Bible college." They only nodded. They seemed to have known all along.

---

Brian C. Stiller is president of Tyndale University College and Seminary in Toronto. He has also served as president of Youth for Christ and of the Evangelical Fellowship of Canada. He has authored ten books, of which his latest include *Preaching Parables to Postmoderns* and *Jesus and Caesar: Christians in the Public Square*. Born and raised in Saskatchewan, he currently resides in Toronto. He has been married to Lily for more than forty-five years.

# Christ in the Room
*~ Philip Marchand ~*

It is embarrassing to admit that some cheesy television program was instrumental in my returning to faith as an adult. One evening—I cannot recall the precise year, but it was in the late 1970s—I chanced to see an episode of a six-part television series entitled *Moses the Lawgiver*, a British-Italian production starring Burt Lancaster as Moses. It was the episode in which Moses is called by God to return to Egypt.

I should explain that at that point I had spent the better part of a decade living in a neo-Freudian therapeutic cult in Toronto trying to liberate my psyche from the neurotic inheritance of oppressive parenting. It wasn't a terrible cult, it was just a very seventies phenomenon. It gave one the sensation of delving ever deeper into the depths of the unconscious, uncovering ever-more-pervasive traumas. It seemed like the process would never end, but one could congratulate oneself on being a psychic explorer.

The fateful televised episode in itself, as I have indicated, was no artistic monument. Leonard Maltin calls the theatrical version of the series, entitled simply *Moses*, "below average." Another critic of the series, I remember, compared it unfavourably to Cecil B. DeMille. But, in fact, it is unfair of me to call the series "cheesy." For one thing, the late novelist Anthony Burgess co-authored the script, and he was no slouch in the writing game. More to the point, the episode itself was sufficiently convincing in its dramatization of God calling on his servant to do his will to awaken some dormant part of my soul. The effect of watching that episode was a hunger aroused, a vision perceived, a flame kindled which flickered weakly for a long time afterwards but never went out.

I should note that I had a Catholic upbringing, which I resolutely rejected after a couple years in university in favour of hippie radicalism and then the teachings of Sigmund Freud

and Wilhelm Reich and Edmund Bergler, as interpreted by
Lea Hindley-Smith, a lay therapist and the matriarch of the
cult I have referred to. All that upbringing, in the late 1960s,
just seemed to drop away as painlessly and effortlessly as snow
melting off a roof in springtime. But the upbringing was sufficiently long-lasting in its effects to allow me no doubt of the
form of the faith I would adopt when I did become serious
about Christianity, via the God who spoke to Burt Lancaster. I
became a practising Catholic again.

I sometimes think there are two poles involved in the
practice of my Catholic Christian faith, poles that date back to
my earliest introduction to religion and which abide today. In
the beginning, those two poles were represented by a book,
the *Baltimore Catechism*, and by an experience, the celebration
of the Mass.

Throughout the decade of the 1950s I spent a good part
of Saturday mornings sitting in the pews of my parish church
being drilled by a nun in the question-and-answer format of
the catechism. Nowadays this is considered a dreadful form
of pedagogy. I rather liked it, however, because I had a good
memory. Also, the structure of the catechism was congenial to
my mind. I love precise definition and the catechism was full
of that. What is the definition of prudence? (No, prudence is
not the same thing as caution.) What is the difference between
sacraments and sacramentals? ("Sacramentals excite in us pi-
ous dispositions, by means of which we may obtain grace.")

When I was twenty years old and reading all the wrong
books—books about existentialism, books about eastern
philosophy—I was more or less ashamed of my predilection
for precise definition. Definitions were rigid, static, narrow-
minded. They did not go with the flow.

Back in the 1950s, meanwhile, the other pole of my
religious practice, the pole of experience as represented by
attendance at Mass, seemed scarcely more suited to withstand

the assault of alien gods. In my young life, the countless hours
I spent at Sunday Mass were hours of boredom. The only thing
that seemed to register in this experience was the reading of
the Gospels in English. Those readings imprinted great swaths
of the New Testament deep into my brain. They didn't cover the
whole of the four Gospels—I read the other bits later. But it
was enough. It was enough that I can now say I know the Gospels more thoroughly than I know any other book in the world.

These two poles of my religious practice, the strictly literary and the experiential, continued to do their work on the
road back to faith. Of the two, the literary was initially most
important. Books gave me intellectual permission to pursue
my journey to faith.

G.K. Chesterton's were the first, in the early 1980s; his
cheerful metaphysics blew aside the fogs of commonplace
thought. Other authors were not Christian but they did yeo-
man service in the cause of truth. *Time and Western Man*, by
Wyndham Lewis, the great modernist painter, novelist, and
critic, for example, proved to be the antidote to the poison of
the French philosopher Henri Bergson, whom I had read as an
undergraduate and who practically patented the notion of going with the flow. (Bergson's god was the Life Force.) Specifically Christian testimony, meanwhile, was offered by the great
medievalist Etienne Gilson, whose book, *The Spirit of Medieval
Philosophy*, revealed the luminous coherence and reasonable-
ness of medieval schoolmen such as St. Thomas Aquinas.

The process is crystallized in my mind by a memory of
taking a train from Ottawa to Toronto with a copy of *Fifteen
Sermons Preached before the University of Oxford*, by John Henry
Newman, which I had just bought in a secondhand bookstore
in Ottawa. On that train, I had an experience that I doubt I
will ever have again—the experience, as we used to say in
the sixties, of having my mind blown. The book as a whole
was responsible for this experience, but chiefly the sermon

entitled "Explicit and Implicit Reason." This sermon was a de-
scription of how our mind actually works, and has since saved
me innumerable hours of reading cognitive scientists clearing
their laborious path to the same point Newman reached, with
infinitely more grace, in the mid-nineteenth century. This experience, you might say, was a nice bonus for having seen that
episode of *Moses the Lawgiver*.

All this literary exploration—adding flesh and blood to
the dry bones of the *Baltimore Catechism*—was exhilarating and
necessary. But that work is largely done, and now more and
more I find the other pole of religious practice, the experiential, to be crucial. What I took for granted as a boy, the celebration of the Mass, has now become in my heart a fantastic
privilege, an undeserved blessing.

The sense of this privilege is often sharpest when travelling and attending Mass in the company of total strangers.
The accents in which the Mass in these unfamiliar churches
is said, even when the language is English, may vary widely.
I remember one Sunday when I was looking for a church in
Victoria, Texas. I was given proper directions and found the
address but was puzzled because I saw no steeple in the vicin-
ity. It turned out the Mass was being held in a basement hall,
where a tall black man in green robes stood in front of rows
of folding chairs. His name was Father Gabriel Otoo and he
was from South Africa. After someone read the first verse of a
psalm I was startled by a sudden cannonade of drumming and
a burst of music like the overture to a Wayne Newton ballad
at the Stardust Resort, coming from a little band, complete
with snare drums, congas, and trumpets, in the corner. The
congregation then sang the psalm response and raised their
arms as they sang, and I realized I was at a "charismatic Mass,"
a Catholic version of a Pentecostal service. Like a Pentecostal
minister, Father Otoo delivered a lively but interminable sermon. The Mass also seemed to go on forever, especially

toward the end when people were introduced to the applause of the congregation because they were celebrating their birthday.

In New Orleans one Sunday—this was before Katrina—I attended Palm Sunday Mass at St. Augustine's, built in 1842 and still the heart of black Catholic life in that city. Its pastor, Father Jerome G. LeDoux, wearing a cinnamon-coloured dashiki, rode to church, in imitation of Our Lord, on the back of one of those mules that pull carriages full of tourists around the French Quarter. The congregation waved palm fronds and sang hymns. The rest of the service was more restrained than Father Otoo's celebration of the Mass, but I remember that the kiss of peace lasted forever, or at least until every member of the congregation had hugged or kissed every other member of the congregation.

It's not just particularly colourful celebrations of the Mass that come to mind, however. I remember a Polish priest saying Mass on Christmas Eve in a tiny chapel in the woods of Gabriola Island, British Columbia. My mother was there, ninety-three years old, having come all the way from her home in a retirement community in Lenox, Massachusetts, to celebrate Christmas with my wife's family. Her mind was starting to fail, and she died a year and a half later. To remember that we were there together on that occasion, one of the last experiences we would truly share, means a world of difference to me.

With all these people, in Gabriola Island, in Texas and New Orleans, there was a bond that had nothing to do with "celebrating community" or even "celebrating our faith." The teenagers at the charismatic Mass wearing green T-shirts and singing a rap song, the parishioners praying with Father LeDoux over an altar consisting of the trunk of a cypress tree, the worshippers inside the chapel in British Columbia trying, not very successfully, to sing Christmas carols, were all gathered for the same purpose. G.K. Chesterton once remarked on the difference between Yahweh pervading the universe and Jesus Christ walking into the room. We were all there, at the Mass, to meet Christ as he entered the room, to obey his command to eat his body and drink his blood, as a foretaste of the heavenly banquet in which we would be far more closely united.

And at the end we were bidden by the priest to go in peace and serve the Lord—the same commandment I saw God giving to Moses, in that long-ago television series.

---

Philip Marchand is film critic for the *Toronto Star* and author of several books, including *Marshall McLuhan: The Medium and the Messenger*, *Ripostes: Reflections on Canadian Literature*, and *Ghost Empire: How the French Almost Conquered North America*. He lives in Toronto with his wife.

# Sorrow and the Wild

# The Aspens
~ *Rudy Wiebe* ~

My mother labelled two other pictures in March 1947, but neither of them is of the funerals. They seem typical homestead work pictures, but as I study them over days they change, they begin to slip from focus to focus, as if these ordinary Brownie Box snaps were shape-shifting.

One was taken in our yard; half the picture is blank snow and a quarter is poplar and spruce sticking up into blank sky; on the narrow band between the two lies a long pile of logs, as high as a man, which is being sawn into firewood. Six men labour around a stationary steam engine that plumes a white cloud against the far spruce: two men lift each log, pass it to two others who shove it against the saw blade, while the fifth seizes the cut block and throws it behind him on the growing heap of firewood; the sixth man—from his shape and the cap pulled low over his ears it must be my father—seems to be coming toward the camera, walking away from the workers. My big brother Dan, legs wide apart and arms cocked in lifting, is unmistakable against the white burst of steam. Who the other men are or who owns the saw outfit I don't know.

The saw blade, hidden by the working men, would be a metre in diameter and spinning so fast one cannot see its teeth. On and on through the winter afternoon its screams burst in the wood. The sawdust heaping up below will be used to cover the fresh ice already cut and hauled from the slough and stacked in our ice cellar dug into the ground behind the house to keep our cream cool for shipping throughout the coming summer; the woodpile Dan will split block by block—Pah will be gone, looking for work and a house in Coaldale—in the lengthening light of spring thaw, and Liz and I will stack the pieces in neat rows to dry. Next winter this great mound will all be burned, it will warm the house for Dan and Isola throughout the bitter cold: it will become fire, this white poplar, *Populus tremuloides,* trembling aspen.

You can hear trembling aspen leaves shiver. At the slight-
est breeze the dark green leaves flicker into their underside
paleness and a sigh like great sorrow flows through the forest.
In that distant picture of the long stack of logs being sawn I
feel something strange, a perception that refuses to focus, but
in the close-up of the other picture my mother labelled in
1947, a gradual recognition emerges.

Our strongest horses, mismatched grey Silver and brown
Jerry, their heads cocked to hold the traces taut on the
whiffletree, are hitched to a bobsleigh piled high with poplar
logs. Dan balances forward on the logs, tall and powerful with
the two reins in one fist and the other arm bent, ready to lift;
behind him our father stands tilted sideways, peering down,
content as ever to be a labourer on his own land, expecting
nothing.

But now, looking, it is the thick, knobbly logs with their
axed ends thrust at me, each of them moments before living
trees, chopped down by my father and brother as they stood
with their sap frozen in their veins waiting for the spring sun,
it is the long poplars with their tips dragging in snow behind
the sleigh that quiver in my mind. This is more than simply the
endless human labour of survival in the Canadian boreal forest: poplar forests grow from Canada to Russia to England and
Israel (*Populus alba*, or *libneh* in Hebrew), and ancient legend
has it that aspens around the circle of the earth have been
trembling since that moment when the hands and feet of Jesus
were nailed to a poplar cross, when his flesh was smashed
against its wood. No aspen trunk will ever again grow straight
enough to form a cross, and the heart-shaped leaves on their
narrow stems will never again stop shivering, for shame, for
endless, endless sorrow.

Stories create feeling beyond reason or guilt; in story we
understand, even as we hear and sense it, that wind can be an
image of the divine moving within us. When wind runs high in

the crowded aspens, we see them bend their thin, pale bodies down again and again like homage, like worship, and we hear and see their flat-stemmed leaves shiver as they turn their whiteness into sighing, groaning together. The long sound of creation, grieving. And sometimes too they do not straighten up again but remain bowed; the youngest, tallest, will grow year after year bent round until their tips touch the earth. And even stooped in such sorrow, in shame and respect and adoration, they also declare themselves unendingly alive: chop down as many poplars as you will, clear any field to the last stick or twig from the surface and out of their roots searching everywhere through the earth new shoots will push up; year by year you will have to labour to contain them at the edges of your field. In fact, scientists tell us that clones of a single aspen seed can occupy up to eighty hectares of land, literally thousands of trees growing through thousands of years from one seed on land first exposed to sun and wind when the Pleistocene ice sheet melted here 12,000 years ago.

The aspen in Canada's boreal forest are the largest living organisms growing on the earth; every one a link in our boundless circle of life.

Perhaps that is why—who can explain how—the death of Jesus for me always was, and will always remain, indelibly more than an historic act of brutal execution. When aspens bend, sighing pale, my body feels fact beyond any sight, or hearing; or denial.

That contradictory, unfathomably comforting awareness: the fire that burns in the soul like ice, the ice like fire.

---

Rudy Wiebe is the author of nine novels and several anthologies, story collections, and works of non-fiction. He won the Governor General's Literary Award for fiction for *The Temptations of Big Bear* (1973) and *A Discovery of Strangers*

(1994), and the Charles Taylor Prize for his memoir *Of This Earth: A Mennonite Boyhood in the Boreal Forest*. In 2003 he became an Officer of the Order of Canada. He lives in Edmonton.

# Vacancy
*~ Diane Tucker ~*

How can you be gone from the world,
from all creation, when even the dog
is still a someone, looking out at me
through her sad, wet-chestnut eyes?

Nature abhorring a vacuum, all the space
you took in the world is now filled,
presumably, with air, with dust and dog hair
and the sound waves of my father's weeping.

It's unfair: even your clothes retain
their substance; your jewelry too,
bathed in your laughter, covered still
with fingerprints you pressed on at the mirror
that must be imprinted with your image
somewhere behind the hindering silver.

The last kiss I gave your wax-smooth forehead
is gone too, then, isn't it? There was no *you*
there to receive it. I kissed the cover
of the beautiful ornate box that carried you.
I kissed it just once after it was empty.

The resurrection of the body is inked
on our deepest pages: after your last
juddering breath I kept holding your hand.
After my father felt for your heartbeat
and shook his head, I placed my fingertips,
expecting the small, sharp jump of a pulse
in your slack and tender wrist.

We waltz through the world breathing
and beating, stupefied somehow by the pulse
of our own rushing blood, its music
a white noise, a refrigerator hum we notice
only when we hear the silence and look up.

---

Diane Tucker's poetry appears in many journals and anthologies, and in her two poetry books: *Bright Scarves of Hours* (Palimpsest Press, 2007) and *God on His Haunches* (Nightwood Editions, 1996). She also works as an English tutor and a freelance editor. She lives in Burnaby, British Columbia. Her website is: www.dianetucker.info.

# Breathe
~ *Joanne Gerber* ~

Surfacing, Annelise is aware mostly of cold. Of being cold. Her
fingers are dusky. Dusky, a term she learned when her son was
in neonatal intensive care, years back. Dusky, you need oxygen.
She needs it. Has it, though she has been trying to hold the por-
celain mask to her face for half an hour now. Her hands palsied,
teeth chattering, legs and arms pneumatic with the waves of
shock. Concentrating, trying to order her breathing, she wills
the oxygen into herself, deep, deeper, into her cramped thigh
muscles, her chilled hands and feet, into her bluish toenails then
up into the high-altitude emptiness of her head.

Altitude isn't the problem, no, the high Himalaya headi-
ness is an illusion. She is elevated only on a pillow sinking into
a waterbed, the bedroom in a bungalow in Regina, Saskatchewan, Canada. The bungalow one scant block from the flat-
open prairie, a sea of grasses and grains. She can imagine no
place more solidly earthbound, closer to planetary base camp.

She pictures herself on her back in that ocean of grass.
The ground is ridged, corrugated, stubble pricks through her
silk shirt—she hasn't dressed for the outing and becomes
aware of the possibility of cacti inconspicuous as landmines
underfoot, will have to walk bare-soled out of this imagining
with great care.

She sees herself walking, gingerly. Sage stings her nostrils,
the back of her throat, as the grass stirs, susurrant, in response
to a small wind.

The sun. Yes, there would be sun. Gentle heat spreads
through her, breaks over her skin like warm bathwater, washes
her. The shaking begins to subside, in freeze-frame moments first,
then sweet lengthening stretches, until just this fine occasional
trembling, trembling, then lissomeness, a blissful benediction in
her limbs. She reaches for the oxygen regulator, dreamily, her
fingers almost pink again, and slowly turns the dial.

Waits.

Dreams.

The hiss of air diminishing, diminishing, becoming a whisper, diminishing—gone. She waits a moment more, concentrates. Yes, the shuddering has passed, her body is allover stillness. She twists the valve to secure the cylinder.

She settles, stretches. Gives herself over to the waterbed.

Lets herself float.

Drift.

Breathe. Slow, unmiserly, luxuriant breaths. She is oxygen rich. The shock has passed, Hallelujah.

Half an hour elapses. Things become sharper, focused, as though a mental f-stop has been reset. Annelise comes back to herself, remembers clearly the panicky sensation of having climbed too far without an air bottle—a waking dream, a delusion from which she is now truly wakened.

Attitude, she acknowledges belatedly, attitude was the problem. She brought this crisis, this being-in-shock on herself. Out front, her car is beached haphazardly, straddling both driveway and juniper shrubs, driver's door probably open, she can't remember kicking it shut behind her, how could she have kicked it? She can remember trying to open it, in the Northside Mall parking lot.

Her breath ghastly, knees watery, hands doing an erratic St. Vitus's dance so that the key jittered past the narrow, the microscopically narrow keyhole, mocking her, a fine frantic scratching against the door. She was dying. Literally. Felt herself shutting down, ice water lapping at her extremities as her blood pressure plunged. Knew that she must call someone before the surge of adrenal energy subsided, must not leave this parking lot alone, must not isolate herself in her car.

Call whom? Annelise would never call out to anyone. She had come all the way outside to the parking lot without alerting a soul.

When the first wave hit, she had been sitting in a ladies' shop
dressing room, on the other side of a mirrored door from any
number of women who might dial 911 for her: saleswomen,
customers—mothers and grandmothers and maybe even off-
duty nurses—but she had cringed and said nothing, her self-
consciousness overriding her survival instincts. She could not
make herself conspicuous, could not cry out, could not force
so much as a whimper of warning. Her tongue was bronze.
Lead. Welded in place.

She shivered, shook her head. She was sliding inexorably
toward oblivion. A card in her wallet listed the deadliest of
her allergies, a card meant to save her from the misguided
ministrations of paramedics. But zippered away like that, the
card would be found too late, after they had tried to stabilize
her with lidocaine. *Severe allergies & multiple chemical sensitivi-
ties: Novocaine*, they would read belatedly. And *sulphite and
phenol preservatives* (the lidocaine suspension). *Alcohol* and
*adhesives* (the needle site), *latex* (their gloved hands), *plastics
and petrochemicals* (the mask they'd have affixed to her face, the
tubing through which the oxygen had snaked). Her Medic-
Alert card would absolve them of blame, nothing more. She
should have thought to keep it in a pocket. She should have
bought a hypoallergenic bracelet.

She should never have left the house unaccompanied.

She felt herself spiralling deeper into the reaction. And
deeper. She was growing colder, shockier, by the moment.

*Pray.*

She did, fervidly.

*Move.* Before her limbs and wits abandoned her altogether.

She decided to make for her car, for home, for her bed,
wounded-animal instinct. She gathered herself.

*Get going.*

Grace: her feet were still operational.

The waves of shock mounted as she moved through the

lava-lamp shimmer of the mall. Curious looks, but no intervention.

At the exit doors, telephones tantalizing as a fleet of life rafts. *9-1-1. Salvation. Call 911.*

But she could not get her purse open.

Could not.

And still not. And still, the effort of clasp and zipper costing her too much air, things becoming vague, her wallet and the vital phone call a mirage now on the horizon of consciousness.

*Annelise!* She pulled herself back into the moment. Teeth chattering, hands clutching invisible netting, she gestured toward the phones, tried to ask a woman for a quarter. Her tongue was lead. Words mimetic. The woman, affronted, looked at her through armadillo eyes. By the alchemy of contempt Annelise became a drunk, indigent, mendicant, a sad, sad case.

Tears. *Please*, she whispered, *9-1-1*.

The woman stepped around her. No quarter.

Annelise shrank, turned, made crookedly for the parking lot. While she was still lucid, get to her car. *Row E. Silver Toyota, Row E.*

Scanning to estimate the distance, she stopped, amazed. Across the tarmac, in the farthest reaches of the lot, a carnival. A candy-cane big top, life-size Coney Island Carousel, a silver Scrambler lunging in complicated orbit, a hooded Caterpillar train, ominously tilted Octopus, plodding ponies, mobile Fun House. *A frisson*. Could she be hallucinating? All this?

The spun-sugar smell of caramel corn and candy floss, animal-peanut stink, shrill of hucksters, barkers, archaic mechanical rides, overexcited kids, jitterbug of colours. The unexpectedness—the very complexity and clarity—of it.

She couldn't possibly have conjured this. Be conjuring this. But it's only June, too soon for a carnival. And how had she overlooked it, driving in? How could she have missed a midway, caravans? Had the reaction been coming on, even then? From what trigger?

It didn't matter. If she was taking it in now—if she was questioning it—she was still anaphylactoid, might not escalate toward anaphylaxis. She had a shot at making it home, making it to her oxygen tank, riding this out. But she was squandering seconds.

*Go. Row E.*

*Car. Thank you, thank you.* The brink of tears, back away.

Key. Mercifully shoved into her jeans pocket for easy access.

The lock.

Key again.

Stick shift. Stick shift and clutch. With her legs bucking now, hands borderline insubordinate, she'd need a miracle.

Concentrate. Just as the Toyota lurches out into traffic: *You don't need a quarter for 911. So no wonder that woman …*

Almost there, signs and wonders.

Back on her bed, back, she refuses to relive the trip home: a banked cloverleaf entrance ramp and a cross-lane exit ramp, never mind the hundred-kilometre-an-hour expressway between. Still here she is, floating, intact, the air sweet and plentiful, her limbs supple as lotus stems in pond water.

Lotus stems. Where did that come from?

She does tend to be swamped by sentimentality in the aftermath. Brain chemicals.

Swamped too, by guilt: in the aftermath, her mood invariably veers toward self-accusation.

Take today. Forget that she survived—that's accidental. How foolish she'd been going to Northside in the first place. The outing was frivolous, as arrogantly risky as a leap from a building. From the pinnacle of a temple. Jesus himself had refused that infernal suggestion. Refused. Yet she, Annelise, has recklessly put the Lord Her God to the test. By going to the mall. Unaccompanied.

Her children might have found her collapsed in the driveway, the police might have been summoned to her crash site on the highway, paramedics might have worked her over on a public bench. Worse, she might have injured someone else— she had endangered dozens of unwitting drivers. Because, frustrated by confinement, inspired by something she had read, she'd presumed on divine protection, immunity from her own folly.

It had seemed a small step of faith, beforehand: the just-one-store, just-one-item, just-one-stab-at-normalcy mission. Faith or presumption, though? Presumption or faith? The question a circular track, already as familiar as the one that the parking-lot ponies must inscribe and re-inscribe even in their dreams, but a track she has only just begun to circumnavigate.

She will have years.

Years. According to the allergists, immunologists, and clinical ecologists, the diagnosticians and prognosticators, the medical magi.

For her foreseeable future, the most ordinary act will be perilous. Trying to maintain her life, she will be forced to make judgment calls with potentially grave consequences. *Walking on water or kayaking after dark in the shipping lanes? Faith or presumption—presumption or faith?*

That's what she'll be asking herself. Every time she leaves her house. Opens the door. Opens the window. Breathes unfiltered air. Every time she lifts food to her mouth. Performs the most seemingly ordinary act.

She flinches, cannot bear to entertain this thought. Cannot.

For the moment, shrugs it off; she has survived this bout. Rolls onto her side, a position that takes concentration.

Brain chemicals, she chides herself. She is freighting a shopping trip with theological significance.

But can't help herself. Her brain ticks on. This is how the chemicals work. How she works.

If moved today by anything beyond simply wanting a new pair of pants, a pair that didn't imply anorexia, she was challenging and charting her limitations. Trying to take the measure of her world. Which seems to be shrinking with the same sickeningly cataclysmic speed as had the universe back in first-year astronomy and geophysics, when her professor demonstrated mathematically that it was elliptical.

The universe, elliptical.

And what was beyond it, seventeen-year-old Annelise had cried out, if it had edges, a shape? What could be beyond the universe without diminishing it so that it was no universe at all, but something infinitely less?

"Other universes," her professor had said, kindly. Titters—the lecture hall full of arts majors like herself trying to finagle the required single science credit with minimal damage to their GPAs.

"Then it's still not the universe you're talking about, sir. No one can measure the universe. Or even imagine their way past it."

"Young lady, I suspect that our contention is semantic, not substantive. Let's leave *definitions* to our colleagues in the humanities, shall we?"

Face aflame, she'd fled the lecture hall with the image of something transparent, gelatinous, ovoid, entrapping her. Had imagined her hands on the quivering universal walls, trying to push them back, determined to stretch them somehow.

In her dreams, for at least a year afterward, the cosmos had been reduced to a silvery amniotic sac. Vast but vulnerable. The ever-present spectre of rupture. Or shrinkage.

And now. As Environmental Illness, Multiple Chemical Sensitivity, Total Allergy Syndrome, Twentieth-Century Disease—this medical enigma—encroaches, is she trying to keep the shrinking cosmos from smothering her by refusing to accept her limitations? (By refusing to accept that the disease even exists? That her immune system has run amok, is attacking her?)

She shudders, sends a small temblor just under the surface of the alabaster sheets.

Another lap of the circuit. It had felt like courage, buckling on her sandals for the outing against all orders. It had felt like a vote of confidence in God, maker of heaven and earth, of her own beset body. But which took more grit, the grand defiant gesture, or digging in for the siege? Trying to outwit—or resolving to outlast—this pernicious onslaught?

Incredibly, she might have died this afternoon. Died. Might yet, next time. Better that than surrender to a living death, is that what she thought? What she thinks?

She hardly knows what she thinks—what *to* think—about what is happening to her.

⁊

"What happened?? The car—" The front door crashing open.

"It's okay. I'm in here." Bracing herself.

"You went out??" Behind Iain's anger, she reminds herself, fear.

As he rushes into the bedroom, his lips and cheeks are chalky. "What was so urgent it couldn't wait until I got home? Until I could go for you?"

She can't begin to go into the larger issues, her real reasons, not with Iain all the way across the room, castigating her with his eyes. They'd need to be lying side by side, bodies just quieted, her hand tracing his collarbone, his hand still warm on her thigh. When did they last lie like that?

"There's a carnival, it came early this year," she tells him. "You should take Noel and Matt."

"You went to *Northside*? Did you buy something?"

She shakes her head.

"So the whole trip was a—" His expression goes unconvincingly neutral and he manages to resist preaching at her—for the moment.

She could tell him about the biblical woman whose story moved her this morning, moved her out the door and into the car. How could Iain argue with that, with her stepping out in faith? (How could she, though, rationalize the near-disastrous outcome? Or open her inner life to scrutiny, when her outer has become the subject of endless dissection and discussion?)

She's so tired.

"But I saw the carnival," she says brightly. "Ponies. Parking-lot ponies, but still ..."

"Bony and saddle-sore, obviously underfed. I saw them on my way to the bank. Poor things looked pathetic. Starved. Just begging to be put out of their misery. There ought to be a—" He sees her disbelief and chokes, realizing. He drops onto the bed, reaches out to her as she rides the shockwaves. His hand on the unpadded blade of her hip.

When he speaks at last, his voice is gentle, "No, you're right, honey. The main thing is nothing happened. I just—You know I didn't mean—"

She closes her eyes.

"I'll go and straighten the car, then, before the boys get home."

He rises, hesitates, moves slowly toward the doorway. There will be no sermon. Not this evening, not tomorrow, not next week. Like so much else, they will never speak of this incident again.

When he is gone, she rolls over.

Into the midst of the sunburnt field, bathed in swaying flaxen light.

She begins to trace, rib by rib, the unpadded cage over her heart.

Float.

Drift.

Breathe.

---

Joanne Gerber, Literary Arts Consultant for the Saskatchewan Arts Board, is a writer, writing instructor, and fiction editor. Her first book, *In the Misleading Absence of Light*, a short story collection, won three Saskatchewan Book Awards, the Jubilee Award for Short Fiction, and was shortlisted for the Toronto Book Award. She has collaborated with composer David L. McIntyre on a chamber opera and song cycle, and has written for stage. She is currently working on a novel, *Like Manna*, and living in Regina.

# The Holes in Our Old, Old Stories

(for PKA)
~ *Daniel Coleman* ~

## Summer 2007

"Newcomers should adapt to Canadian ways when they come here, as our fathers did—leave the past behind, start afresh. When I go to another country, I adapt to the people, I don't expect them to adapt to me. We make too many concessions—turbans on our police, *sharia* in our suburbs, courts replaced by sentencing circles, no more prayer in schools. We've lost our pride, our founding values, have to whisper we're Canadian."

## Spring 1763

Lord Jeffrey Amherst, Commander-in-Chief of British North America, to Colonel Henry Bouquet, during Pontiac's uprising: "Could it not be contrived to send the *Small Pox* among those disaffected tribes of Indians? We must on this occasion use every stratagem in our power to reduce them."

William Trent, Commander, militia of the town of Pittsburgh, journal entry for May 24: "We gave them two Blankets and an Handkerchief out of the Small Pox Hospital. I hope it will have the desired effect."

## Fall 1982

A Cree Pentecostal minister is pulled over by the RCMP on Broad Street in Regina, Sunday, 8 a.m. The streets are empty.

"Where you headed, Mister?"

"Morning, Officer. Full Gospel Chapel. I'm the pastor."

"No shit. Show me your ID. You look kinda wrinkled. Been out drinkin', buddy? Good communion wine? Sweet grass for the flock? Spread 'em, bud, I gotta pat you down."

### 1867 to 2007

In days of yore, O Canada, God saved our gracious King. From Britain's shore, by dawn's early light, Wolfe the dauntless hero saved the True North strong and free. He was victorious, happy and glorious, and planted firm Britannia's flag on Canada's fair domain. Here may it wave, glorious and free, and joined in love together—the thistle, shamrock, rose entwined, the home of the brave, the Maple Leaf, O Canada, forever!

Oh, say, can you see?

### Winter 1890, as told in 1980

"When Great-Grandpa and his brothers topped the ridge near the Red Deer and squinted at the glare of snow, they thought—city boys from Denmark—the tufts of grass breaking through drifts meant black loam. They did! The tufts meant loam! But it took two summers dredging ditches before they could walk instead of row from hut to hut. They had three years to prove up, so they settled their wives and kids into sod huts they had made with soft, white hands on the highest hillocks. Can you imagine, trying to keep house with swamp rot as your floor?"

### Fall 2006

Afternoon sun slants through the blinds in my office, where a serious young man from a Christian college fixes me with clear blue eyes. He's in his first year of graduate school, and yesterday a young professor told him there's no place in our field for faith-based work. He knows I disagree, and his question tests my hue on the religious spectrum: "Professor Coleman, would you say we Christians are an oppressed minority in Canadian universities—in Canada as a whole?"

## Fall 2006

A week before, Peter sat with me in this same room. Born in
Lagos, schooled in Bristol, then U. of T. More than once I've
seen him asked where he comes from.

"Toronto. Where are *you* from?"

"No, I mean, where are you *really* from?"

"I moved with my family to Toronto from Bristol. Where
are you *really* from?"

He's a dancer, Baptist, poet, artist of the spoken word,
and he just moved here to start his PhD. At the sight of his
fetching black face and nappy groomed hair, the first landlady
shook her head: "No drugs in my house." He persisted, found
a place on the ground floor of a brick heritage home, left one
load, and went back to Toronto for another. When he and
his dad returned next day, his clothing had been jerked from
closets, boxes, drawers, tossed out the window, his books
and papers strewn around the room. The intruders had torn
his shirts, his sheets, his underwear, urinated on his clothing,
scratched a crude swastika on the floor.

| | |
|---|---|
| 9:00 a.m. | Peter calls police. He and dad wait outside—not to disturb evidence. |
| 9:05 | Peter calls landlord at work. |
| 11:30 | Landlord comes by on lunch. |
| 11:45 | Landlord calls police. Again. |
| 12:30 | Landlord returns to work. Says to call and let him know. |
| 2:30 | Peter calls police. Again. He and dad still outside. |
| 4:30 | Landlord comes by after work. Calls police. Again. Says he'll release Peter from his lease. |
| 4:45 | Peter and dad walk in, take pictures, clean up, leave. |

The police never come. Later, a lawyer tells Peter he should have reported a Hate Crime, not a Break and Enter. Hate Crime's got a special unit, he says. They'd be right there. They've got fifty-sixty B&E's a day—you're lucky if they ever come.

## 1909
Charles William Gordon, Presbyterian minister, a.k.a. "Ralph Connor," bestselling author, speaking in the voice of Reverend Brown, missionary to a Ukrainian colony on the South Saskatchewan, in his novel *The Foreigner*: "These people here exist, an undigested foreign mass. They must be digested and absorbed into the body politic. They must be taught our ways of thinking and living, or it will be a mighty bad thing for us in Canada. My main line is the kiddies. I can teach them English, and then I am going to doctor them, and, if they'll let me, teach them some elements of domestic science; in short, do anything to make them good Christians and good Canadians, which is the same thing."

## Winter 2007
Signing a security certificate allows the Minister of Public Safety to detain people designated as security risks. Charges need not be read against them, they may not meet with legal counsel, they do not qualify for bail, the Minister is not obliged to say why they're detained. Under this measure, Mahammad Mahjoub has been in prison for seven years; Mahmoud Jaballah, six years; Hassan Almrei, six years in solitary confinement; Mohammed Harkat, five years; and Adil Charkaoui, four years. None of these men has ever come to trial. In February, the Supreme Court determined that security certificates violate the Charter of Rights and Freedoms. But the court suspended this judgment for a year, so Parliament will have time to put a new law in its place.

**Fall 2007**

I consider those clear blue eyes and how I go quiet when my
love for God gets blasted, yet again, for the Indulgences, the
Crusades, Copernicus's crushed telescope—not to mention
residential schools and those burning White House Bushes.
I plumb my tiresome mix of pride and shame, and think it's
time we drank the cup of our whole history; listened to, not
surfaced over, the holes in our old, old stories.

---

Daniel Coleman lives in Hamilton, Ontario, where he is a
professor and Canada Research Chair in the Department of
English and Cultural Studies at McMaster University. He has
published scholarly books on Canadian literature and a memoir called *The Scent of Eucalyptus* about growing up as the child
of missionaries in Ethiopia. His book *In Bed with the Word: Reading, Spirituality, and Cultural Politics* is forthcoming in 2009.

# Atomic Birthday
~ *Sally Ito* ~

On the day your daughter turns six, you are travelling with
her to Hiroshima to the Peace Museum. The sleek white bullet
train goes so fast you hardly notice the buildings, the train stations that pass in a blur. You have not been there in years; you
wonder if it has changed. The first time you went you were
single, not yet twenty, travelling the country in search of your
"roots," and people said you should go there—not people you
knew, like your relatives, but other friends like the Americans,
who dropped the bomb.

It was a hot August day and there were chairs set up in
front of the cenotaph. Pomp and circumstance was about to
unfold. Speech-making and vowing. *Never again. No more Hiroshima.* The controversial prime minister, a right winger and
hawkish, was going to be there.

Phalanxes of policemen in riot gear line the boulevard
behind the museum in case the "peace march" goes awry. You
sit in the very back row with your American friends. They are
more political than you. When the prime minister makes his
speech, they stand up and turn their backs on him. You don't
do anything. You're not sure if you are acting cowardly or are
simply embarrassed.

The next visit to Hiroshima is years later with a friend,
again in the summer. Her mother is from the city, and her
grandparents still live there. You visit the grandparents' home.
You remember the house as spacious and cool. The grandfather is a retired doctor. He loves to play tennis. Again you do
the sights of the city, but for some reason, you do not remember visiting the Peace Museum although you must have. Were
you chatting too much? You remember shopping, and having
coffee. Afterwards, you went to Miyajima Island. The deer
there were so tame. You took pictures of the famous orange
shrine gate in the sea and bought some Japanese maple cakes.

Your friend's mother died of cancer seven years ago. Lymphoma. The only story you hear is how her mother went out looking for the dead the day after. Then a few days later, her hair fell out.

Now your friend and you talk about how little you know of your Japanese mothers' lives. And you think how lucky you are to still have your mother, especially now, this time when you are in Japan, and can still ask and receive answers. She is visiting Japan at the same time as you, staying with her sister in Shiga as your family also has been these past few weeks.

Her visit has been timed with yours because you have decided to write a book about the family—your *Japanese* family. You have brought your children to meet them all, to feel the balm of their kinship and affection. This is your grandmother's country, you tell your daughter, *Baachan*'s land. And here are her siblings—Uncle Hidero, Aunty Yoko, Aunty Michiko.

Hiroshima is a new city, reborn out of the ash. But like so many others, you are pilgrim to its former destruction. There are more foreigners here, more signs in English, French, German, Russian. You step into the tourist information centre. "Where is the Atomic Dome?" you ask. "The Peace Park?" The young woman at the counter pulls out a map. Shows you the spot. Vaguely now, you recall the way. How you had to ride a streetcar. Streetcars were one of the quaint things about the city. They've been updated since your last visit. Some are as long as snakes with that black rubbery accordion between the cars that bends and shifts with the curves in the road. You board one of these fancy ones. Your daughter sits in your lap while your son and husband look out the window. Furtively, your daughter sticks her thumb in her mouth. You pry it out. "You're too old for that," you admonish quietly. Your husband has told her that now she is six, she must stop sucking her thumb.

*Genbaku Doh-mu, Heiwa Koen.* Atomic Dome, Peace Park. That is your stop. You clamber out with other foreigners eager

for the sight. It is a bright, sunny day. You scan the horizon
with your hand on your brow. Ah, there it is. The spindly
barbwire-like frame, the skeletal girders of the dome like
ribs in a skullcap. The children run toward it. You, too, feel a
powerful urgency to get as close as possible to this monumen-
tal ruin, now carefully cordoned off by wrought-iron fencing
and manicured park ground. A group of schoolchildren are in
front of it, drawing it on big white sketchbooks. The teacher
is pointing and gesticulating. Your son wishes he brought his
sketchbook. He, too, would like to draw the stark frame in
raw bold strokes of charcoal.

You walk around the dome, take pictures. Your husband
reads the written plaques. Formerly the Hiroshima Industrial
Promotion Hall, it was built in 1915 and hailed as an archi-
tectural wonder for its time. Located almost directly under
the hypocentre of the blast, it miraculously survived as one
of the few buildings left in the city. In 1996, it was declared a
UNESCO World Heritage Site.

The building has a gaunt, haunted look as if weary of its
desecration. It has had to be repaired in the last decade, refit-
ted with iron girders to support its crumbling frame. Day and
night, it has served as a reminder of the destruction of the past
and has become the focal point for throngs of visitors.

Your children are laughing and chasing one another.
"Where's Daddy?" your daughter runs up to you, breathless.
He is gazing at the river. It is a placid, implacable blue, flowing
smoothly by. You stop to look. It was here at the banks that
people, scorched and parched with thirst, poured into the
waters looking for relief, fire raging all around them, black
smoke filling the air. You tell the children. They nod sombrely.

You walk down toward the cenotaph. It is a sleek cement
archway through which you can see the Atomic Dome. It
houses the peace flame that will only be extinguished when all
nuclear weapons have been abolished. You take a picture here.

Nearby is water flowing out from the fountain in a shallow channel made out of marble. Children are playing there. Your daughter joins them. When you head toward the museum, your daughter lingers. "Mommy," she calls, "Mommy, look at this!" She points to a corner of the channel where a cluster of tadpoles squirm and wriggle in the water. It is an amazing sight for such a sterile environment; you wonder where the frogs were that laid the eggs, where among the concrete and marble they might have spawned.

The Peace Museum is a long rectangular building on posts. School children on their annual June excursions mill around the grounds. You skirt past them to the entrance on the east side of the building. It is fifty yen to enter, the cheapest museum rate you've encountered so far in your travels. Earphones and headsets can take you through the exhibit in several different languages. Volunteer guides are also available. As you enter into the first hall, you hear one of them, an elderly man, telling someone, "You see, that was a building that used to be on the corner. I took a tram past it every day." Those guides were not available when you were here last.

Your husband and son become engrossed in reading the wall panels explaining Hiroshima's history before the war. The documentation is impeccably clear. It outlines the growth of the city as a military port. In your grandfather's memoir that you have been translating with your aunt, he writes of going to Hiroshima to board the army transport that will eventually take him to Indonesia. That was in 1942. Instead of being a soldier, he is with a group of businessman who will exploit the new trade opportunities opened up by the military in this southeast Asian country. He leaves his wife and family, including your six-year-old mother, in Osaka.

Your daughter, now the same age, is too small to read the fine print on the walls. Instead, she is attracted to the middle of the room where a large model reconstruction of the city is displayed. A large red ball representing the bomb hangs above, showing exactly where the bomb was dropped. Your daughter circles the model and peers through the plexiglass walls around it. She knows what the big red ball means. She's heard about the bombs falling and falling out of the bellies of the airplanes that fly at night. Mostly she's heard about it from you. Never from your mother.

A week ago, you and your mother travelled to the village in the mountains on the outskirts of Osaka where your mother evacuated with her family. They left to escape the bombing raids on the city. On one bad night there your grandmother hurriedly took your mother and her siblings to her older brother's place, which had a big storehouse. The storehouse was jammed with other people taking refuge, and her brother could not fit your mother's family in. Your grandmother was angry; that was the last straw. She insisted to her father that they be moved far into the hills away from the city—*kodomo no tame ni*—for the children's sake.

While your daughter wanders around, you read a panel about the student corps who on the day of the strike were working on the riverbank, dismantling old buildings. Since there was a labour shortage, junior high school students were co-opted into working for the military. Your mother's cousin in Osaka worked in such a corps. He did not evacuate with your mother's family. Instead he worked on sites that made him a target for the enemy. "Oh yeah, they flew down and shot at us—bam, bam, bam—it was the scariest moment of my life."

By now, your daughter has joined you. She is quiet and clings to the side of your leg. Timidly, she asks. "Mommy, whose side were we on?" You pause to think. Finally you say, "We're Canadians. And Canada fought on the same side as America."

Your daughter's face crumples in confusion. The words are disturbing. She knows it was America that dropped the bomb. But Canada? How could that be?

"So we're the ones that dropped the bomb on Baachan's country?" She asks incredulous. Her eyes widen, and then suddenly, she bursts into tears. "Baachan, Baachan," she cries, her whole body trembling.

It is too much for her. You scoop your daughter's little body into your arms and carry her to a bench where you can hold her. Gently, you rock her as she blubbers on about Baachan's country, Canada, war, bombing, people dying. Finally, she grows quiet, slips her thumb into her mouth and presses her body against you. Suppressing the urge to pull out her thumb, you simply hold her. You close your eyes. They, too, are moist with tears.

Several hours later you are back at your aunt's house in Shiga. Your mother and she have been waiting up for you. Your aunt has bought your daughter a little present—a toy. "Happy Birthday!" she says. You thank your aunt and then tell of your misgivings on taking your daughter to such a place on such a day. Your aunt shrugs. "It is terrible," she says, "but it is a terrible *truth*, and children should know the truth."

Your mother is at the dining room table, eating some fruit. "We went there, don't you remember?" she says. "Seventeen years ago when you were studying at Waseda University. We went with Aunty Kay on our way down to Kyushu. It was my first time. Aunty Kay's, too." She pauses, then continues. "There were those burnt uniforms and the piles of melted roof tiles and that girl running to the river, her face all blackened, and her skin peeling off ..."

Yes, you remember vividly the museum displays she speaks of, but you have forgotten about this visit you made with your mother so many years ago with your Nisei great-aunt. That was the year your father died. The year he received his redress cheque from the federal government for having been interned as a child in interior British Columbia during the war.

It is a wonder you have forgotten. Ironic, even, given that you are here now taking your own daughter this time for the same reason: namely, *never* to forget, and to know the truth—the many truths—of what happened during the war.

Your mother calls your daughter. Gives her a piece of fruit. "Taste it," she says. "It is good."

---

Sally Ito is a writer and teacher who has published two books of poetry, *Frogs in the Rain Barrel* and *Season of Mercy*, and a collection of short fiction entitled *Floating Shore*. She attends St. Margaret's Anglican Church in Winnipeg, where she resides.

## On Bergman
~ *John Bentley Mays* ~

When death came for film and theatre director Ingmar Bergman in the summer of 2007, it found a lonely old man living
on an island off the Swedish coast, and an artist whose most
important accomplishments lay far in the past. He still had numerous fans, as we were reminded by the outpouring of tributes. But despite the polite homage often paid him by younger
directors, he had no followers in Scandinavia or anywhere
else. And most of his ardent admirers these days, I imagine,
belong to an older generation that witnessed the premieres
of the masterpieces Bergman produced around 1960: *Wild
Strawberries* (1957), *The Seventh Seal* (1957), *The Virgin Spring*
(1960), *The Silence* (1963), and others.

Though I had seen Bergman's films of this period as they
were released, it was only after my immigration to Canada,
in 1969, that I began to understand them. I had come from
America's tumultuous student revolts, racial conflicts, and
protests against the Vietnam War, all of which I had weathered
badly. Arriving in Toronto under the cloud of a severe mental
breakdown, I found that the relative peace of my new Canadian home offered me a much-needed chance to heal, and
also to reflect on recent history and the culture I perhaps too
eagerly devoured in the 1960s. Bergman, especially, began to
make sense to me as he had not before. Coming back to my
senses, and coming back to God at the same time, I found it
possible, at last, to comprehend the depth of Bergman's art of
the human condition, and the breadth of his creative vision.

Though frequently humorous—charming scenes break
through the visual and existential frostiness of *Wild Strawberries* and *The Seventh Seal*, for example—his films were utterly
serious, and devoid of irony. He told his greatest stories with a
few remarkably talented actors—a troupe that included Gunnar
Björnstrand, Max von Sydow, and Liv Ullmann—and seemed
quite able to do without the special effects directors nowadays

find so indispensable. Most important, Bergman used his camera to probe hard topics in human life with penetrating clarity and no pulled punches: the anxiety of facing death, for example, the loss of religious conviction, the ruthless violation of a child's innocence, the disintegration of marriage.

Bergman's themes are, of course, timeless and pressing, and that urgency gives the films freshness that has persisted undimmed down to the present day. But these themes had special meaning for many of us coming of age during the 1960s. The nuclear standoff between the United States and the Soviet Union pressed upon us the threat of imminent death. Traditional values—the integrity of marriage and the family, the moral teachings of religion—were being undermined in Europe and North America by the aggressive hedonism and materialism of post-war culture.

In those days, and ever since, young people were offered a plethora of panaceas to dull the pain of this difficult time: saccharine romance movies, TV sit-coms, and the greedy pleasure of consumerism, Valium, and sexual promiscuity, and, a little later in the 1960s, recreational drugs, various pop "spiritualities," and the utopian promises of the leftist student movement.

One thing compelling about Bergman's cinema in this period was its absolute refusal of all those popular consolations for the dread and hopelessness he felt to be the fate of contemporary humankind. If God and enduring values had withdrawn from the world, as Bergman believed, then the results must be exposed for what they were: dire, desperate, unrelieved. In *Winter Light* (1962), the village pastor is losing his faith, and thus has nothing to say to a troubled fisherman who comes to him seeking spiritual guidance; the fisherman later commits suicide. The elderly professor in *Wild Strawberries* (1957)—played with conviction by the formidable great actor and film director Victor Sjöström is forced by nightmares and chance encounters to acknowledge the futility and meaninglessness of his life.

It's little wonder that Bergman's films were often criti-
cized as gloomy and ponderous—a judgment that only gathered strength as the pleasure-seeking 1960s wore on. For the
Christian and unbeliever alike, however, they had the virtue of
being entirely fearless when it came to setting out the truth of
human life without hope. Bergman chose to portray a world
without God. And, indeed, without God—without the goals
of justice, love, and mercy God commands us to pursue, even
in deepest darkness—the world of human experience is indeed a prison from which there is no hope of parole, a deadly
routine without meaning.

But at the same time that Bergman gave us unforgettable parables of life without God, he also warned his viewers
against accepting any substitute for the God we have lost or
rejected. In film after film, with inexorable force, Bergman
ruthlessly exposes the futility of substitutes ranging from
sexual passion and worldly learning to self-contained indi-
viduality, sentimental piety, even the pleasures of family life.
His admonitions were valid then, and they are valid now. The
hunger for God that God has put in us will only be satisfied by
God. Without God, we are left only with ourselves and our
warring hearts, and the desolation Ingmar Bergman describes
in his brilliant films.

John Bentley Mays is an award-winning Toronto writer on architecture, visual art and design, and general topics in contemporary culture. He is architecture columnist for the *Globe and Mail*,
columnist for the *Catholic Register*, and a frequent contributor
to *Azure*, *Canadian Architect*, *Canadian Art,* and other periodicals.
His books include *Power in the Blood: Land, Memory, and a Southern
Family* and *In the Jaws of the Black Dog: A Memoir of Depression*. He
is currently at work on a book that profiles key shapers of modern Toronto's culture and public life.

# Where Was God?

~ *Joy Kogawa* ~

*Joy Kogawa's novel* The Rain Ascends *tells the story of Millicent Shelby's shattering discovery in middle age that the elderly clergyman father she adores has abused young boys throughout his life. In this excerpt from the book, Millicent recounts one part of her struggle for truth and redemption.*

I first met Kate Middleton, Archdeacon Kate Middleton, in Ragland, about six years ago, a little over two months after my frantic flight to see the bishop. Father and I had been expecting we knew not what—a letter, a summons—some sort of communication. Yet week after week nothing was happening. I was beginning to feel that things might continue as they always had. After all, the church had known years before. Then there were two long-distance calls—one from the church, one from the press. The first was expected; the second was not.

I was tidying the living room when the first call came. Long distance. A prim-sounding voice asked for Canon Shelby.

"He's resting," I said. "I'm sorry. Is there a message?"

"Archdeacon Middleton," the diocesan secretary said crisply, "is driving to the coast and expects to be through Ragland the week of the twelfth. Would Tuesday be possible?"

Promptly at two o'clock on the appointed day, there was a rather tentative knock. I had imagined a male cleric, tall perhaps, thin and austere, and was surprised when I opened the door. The archdeacon was a woman, middle-aged, more stocky than plump, round glasses, her white dog-collar stark and official against her navy blue. She stood, hands together, as Father, his shoes polished, wearing his second-best grey-green suit, shuffled into the living room to meet his interrogator.

"Archdeacon Middleton, this is my father." Her nod was, I thought, curt.

Father eased himself onto the edge of his armchair. He did
not lean back. Neither did she, as she sat opposite him on the
couch, her back straight. If Father was surprised to see a woman
archdeacon, he did not let on. His eyes were wide, childlike.
Whether by intent or not, trust and innocence were declared in
his open gaze. After a brief moment of small talk—the view of
the mountains, the plants in the sunroom that she could see if
she turned—she directed the conversation to other topics. She
knew Eleanor [wife of Millicent's brother Charlie], and had met
her recently again in Calgary at a conference on reconciliation.
In her childhood, she'd often heard "Shelby Selects."

"You're a living legend, Canon Shelby. You have many
admirers." Father shifted uncomfortably and looked down at
the carpet.

We knew why she had come. If Mother were present,
she'd be saying as she so often did, "Cling to God, Barnabas.
Life can be so punishing—so cruel. But that's when we must
cling the hardest. Cling as if your life depended on it."

Archdeacon Middleton, mercifully, was not an imposing
figure. Her efforts to put us at ease were not wasted. I offered
her tea. Perhaps it was her lopsided homey smile, or the ordi-
nariness of teacups, milk and sugar—or perhaps it was the sun
on my arm and Boots batting a dustball at my feet—that made
me begin to feel almost relaxed. No chilling staccato of violins
to signal anything sinister.

"I am here—you know that I have come to talk with you
about—your problem." She was quietly earnest. She asked, as
I had, about his childhood.

Father responded in one-word sentences, his head bowed.

"You were accosted by the neighbour, you say, just once?"
She was frowning as she took out a notepad. It seemed impossible that a single childhood sexual trauma could account for
a lifetime's perversion. She shuffled through what looked like
several pages of notes. I wondered how much the bishop had
conveyed to her.

"We understand so little," she said. "Perhaps you could help us, Canon Shelby."

Father could not help. He could not say the words. It was as if that part of him that remained in civil company could not bridge the gap. Nor could I. The pauses were long as she waited patiently for Father to speak. Had he been sexually oriented toward children all his life?

I could not tell what the intention was for the visit, and what she had been sent to do. It occurred to me briefly, as she glanced back and forth through her notes, that it might be my sanity that was on trial, and that she had come to verify my talk with the bishop. But the thought passed. Clearly, she was trying to understand as much as she could. Beneath her quiet questioning, I could not detect any emotion—neither loathing nor pity. She could have been asking for the time of day.

"How do you think of your sexuality—if you, say, compare it ...?"

I doubted that Father ever thought of himself as so different from others. One's sexuality was a private matter after all, was it not? People did not talk about such things.

She did not press for more than he could say. She turned to me and her voice was kind as she asked, "You must have thought about all this so much, Millicent. How do you see ...?"

"How do I see the contradictions?"

"Yes. The contradictions, if you like. How do you see your father?"

"I—yes, I have thought about it—and my guess is that—Father, that—that you're still—in so many ways—still just eight years old. You're still locked in that first trauma. Hooked by it."

"Hooked?" she asked.

"Yes," I said, nodding. "Hooked. I think that's the word." There was something so genuinely childlike in Father. He was trusting, excitable, contagiously enthusiastic and so wholehearted. I'd often thought of him as a child in a man's body, a Peter Pan, a boy who never grew up and who spent his lifetime battling Captain Hook in his own never-never land with other lost boys. Could this be Father's story, I wondered aloud—Peter Pan hooked in Captain Hook's embrace, attempting to reconcile an irreconcilable experience?

"You're suggesting that Peter Pan is Captain Hook? And Captain Hook is Peter Pan?" Kate Middleton looked at me quizzically, and at Father, who appeared to be as puzzled as she.

"I—I think I'm saying something like that."

She considered this for a moment, then shook her head slightly and said, "But that's not the story for every lost boy, is it?"

This was Eleanor's point over and over again. "Not all children who are molested become molesters," she'd said. This was the chorus sung in unison by the lawmakers, the justice seekers.

The weight of the argument was a stone in my chest. I would never be able to expel it, however deeply and often I might sigh. It remained undeniable. We are creatures of choice. Where one person sees pearls, another sees pellets of dung, as Father himself used to say. Not all lost boys would choose to become Captain Hooks.

I had spent a lifetime looking for excuses. I was still looking. It had become a way of being.

Father was searching our faces, his eyes beseeching.

Kate Middleton put her notepad and pen away, then quietly, as if to herself, she asked, "In your private devotions, Canon Shelby ... where do you suppose ... where was God?"

Father, hands folded like a schoolboy's, his brow arched in perplexity, lifted his gaze beyond Kate's prayerful face, out past the window, beyond the walls, beyond the hills.

Where was God?

This one great timeless question. Where, for my father, where, for the children, where, for the victims of everyday crimes and crimes unimaginably horrible, was God? And where, today, for the countless children of Abraham who war with each other in rivalry and rage—Christians—Protestants, Catholics—Muslims—Jews—where for the children of poverty and the criminals of wealth, where for the unfeeling hordes of us and the unseen vast legions of the world's victims, where today in the great unforgiven and unforgiving world is God?

In the seeking where there is no finding, in the knocking where no door opens, in the absence where the cry for love is met by betrayal and in that great terrible silence filled with a suffering that knows no solace, where is God? Where are You, my God, my Goddess, at such times, in such places? Where, in the mystery of the absence of love, are You?

Merciful and Abundant One, I know You as the Friend, hidden but not absent, who walks steadfastly with us through the conundrums and mazes and terrors of our unknowing, and through the porous walls between worlds. You lead us as surely as the North Star guides the sailors of the seas, beyond our time-heavy travel to the places where You are. You carry us there, You carry me here, now, to the moving of Your steady, still, wonderful light, Your luminous, warm, becoming everywhere light. You are where love is, as it resides even without creaturely crookedness and our so strange and bent encountering and in our recognition of our hunger for You. You cry that impossible cry within us that the ancient psalmist cried.

"My God, my God, why hast Thou forsaken me?"

Merciful One, You know our utter despair. That cry anchored in the depths of the human heart forms the structure of the bridge between us and You. At the heart of the impossible, in the doorways that lead nowhere, in our incomprehension and in the extremity of our abandonment, You are. In

all that is lost, in all that suffers, You are. In the silence more
than in the speaking, in our dread and in our weeping, You are.
Beyond what I could have dreamed possible, You are.

Beloved Friend, I know You in the love that shone through
my wretched father's life more than in Charlie's or Eleanor's
righteousness and judgments. I know You better in the sinner
than the saint. I glimpse You on the city streets where the
homeless ones lie, and in the dying woods and streams I know
You. And more dearly, more nearly, have I known You in my
plea for mercy than in the great good call for justice. I know
You in the world's many wondrous stories of compassion
as I know You in the One who came as Love and who died,
forgiving and forsaken and broken. In all the hoping, praying,
dreaming, trusting places where light and shadow struggle,
You are. And now in this my every-morning new day, as on
that afternoon six years ago when Father and Kate Middleton
and I searched the skies asking where You were, the question
bearing no judgment, the silence filled with trust. You were
there. You are here.

Kate Middleton's face was peaceful as she acknowledged
the healing balm within the meditative listening that greeted
her question.

In response to my own question about her inner journey,
she tried, as I have also tried since, to explain, stumbling over
her words and laughing at the failure of this clumsy tool we
call language.

"At least start by calling me Kate," she said as I continued
to address her formally as Archdeacon Middleton. She spoke
of the primacy of friendship in her life—her friendship with
the Source of friendship, her radical friendships with the
demonized persons of the day, "who are no more demons than
I am." Friendship, for her, was the most necessary work of our
day—not the easy act of engaging with the like-minded, but
the arduous, world-altering labour of befriending the enemy.

"And this you take to be an archdeacon's task? This is your profession?"

She laughed at the term "professional friendship," calling it an oxymoron.

Father, his eyes closed, leaned back in his armchair as the conversation flowed around him.

"How do you manage to see friends where others see demons?" I asked.

"You've heard the phrase, 'They became what they beheld'?"

I had.

"I think we behold what we are," she said. "We say, 'They this. They that. They. They devour. They are monsters.' And all that venting, all that rage, reflects ourselves. We deflect the horror of what we collectively are doing. Devouring the planet. Devouring the children. Devouring the future."

"We consume because we are consumed? We are consumed by the need to consume?"

"Yes. Yes. But we also love because we are loved."

I didn't know if Father was listening or understanding. He almost seemed to be falling asleep. The Comforter was present to me in Kate Middleton's thoughtful presence. But how the justice-seeking, zero-tolerance church intended to deal with Father, I did not know.

It was as she was preparing to leave that I finally asked, "Could you tell me what we might expect from the church? Father and I?"

She rummaged through her purse for a somewhat worn business card. "Millicent, you must feel free to call me at any time." She wrote her home phone number on the back of the card and handed it to me. "Any time at all." Then, looking from me to Father, who was struggling to stand, and back to me again, she assured us that there would be no public flogging, no tar and feathers, no dragging through the streets—at least, not by the church. A letter would go out to the bishops. We would get a copy. His licence would be revoked.

I walked down the front steps with her to her car. Across the street, an elderly woman from the choir at St. John's glanced over at us. She stopped and waved.

"Lovely day," she called cheerfully. "How is your father, Millicent?"

"Oh, he's all right," I called back a little weakly. "Tired these days, though."

"We miss him in church. Will you tell him?" She glanced curiously at Kate Middleton, a stranger in a clerical collar, who nodded and smiled her lopsided smile. Our friendly, airy gestures, my nonchalant wave, were keeping the secret securely locked away. There would be no introductions today. Should the imps break loose and leap toward the nice, trusting people of St. John's, should the mad mobs get a whiff of the scandal, the sky would turn red with blood.

As she crossed the street toward us, I shrank back. All that was needed was one report. "She's going to find out, isn't she," I whispered. "The whole town will know."

Kate Middleton put a firm hand on my shoulder. "Stand tall, Millicent," she whispered back. "Hold your head up. You hold your head up high."

---

Joy Kogawa is a poet and novelist who divides her time between Vancouver, British Columbia, and Toronto, Ontario. Her semi-autobiographical first novel, *Obasan*, received numerous awards, including the 1982 Books in Canada First Novel Award. She is also the author of the novels *Emily Kato* and *The Rain Ascends*, five books of poetry, and two children's books. She is a Member of the Order of Canada.

# Wild Roses

~ *Peter Short* ~

Much in the spiritual tradition falls into the realm of the
unlikely, because the spiritual tradition has its face turned
toward the living and radiant one. The eyes struggle to see but
from the human point of view, God is so unlikely, so stunning,
sometimes so unsightly and always so impossible. And this is
the way it must be. Or God would not be God at all.

Jonah comes to mind. That Jonah got swallowed and lived
in the belly of a great fish until he got spit out alive on the
beach—not likely.

That the waters of the Red Sea drew back to permit the
Israelites to cross over—not likely.

That Jesus was born of a virgin. Well, you know what Karl
Barth said about that: the great theologian said the virgin birth
is a doctrine posted on guard at the gate of the mystery of
Christmas. No one should think they can hurry past this sentry,
reminding all who enter this region that they set their feet upon
a road at their own cost and risk. The virgin birth is a warning
against walking blithely amongst the demands and dangers of
the gospel. Faith will demand reason all right, but it will demand something deeper than calculation and higher than mental
capacity. It is this greater requirement of faith that causes the
spiritual tradition to fall so often into the realm of the unlikely.

That Jesus was raised from the dead—not likely.

As unlikely you might say as a rose growing red and fragrant in the cold wind of winter. A book title comes to mind:
W.O. Mitchell's *Roses Are Difficult Here*.

And so they are. Roses are difficult in the Canadian
climate in which Mitchell writes and in which we live, every
bit as difficult as lives of kindness and courage and grace are
difficult where you live.

Suppose you had to choose a title for your life and your
work. Suppose you had to say in a phrase what it's like to be

inside your skin and to live the struggle you live. Don't you think that might be a good title? Roses Are Difficult Here.

In my work, day after day I receive stories that would break your heart. People under stress. People alone, lonely, and afraid. People starving for encouragement. People thirsty for a word from the Lord, even in the church where the Lord is a mantra and a motto. People whose lives and work have become a bitter day in December. Roses! Difficult? People are all the time telling me that roses are impossible here.

But here's the thing. It's not problems that steal the life out of you. In fact, when you think about it, you've no doubt overcome many obstacles in your life. It's not stress that turns out the lights in the interior castle. Some of your great and shining moments have happened in the most stressful circumstances.

It's not the presence of problems or the presence of stress that makes roses difficult here. It's not the presence of anything. It's an absence. It's an abandoned and boarded-up heaven. It's the silence of God and the aloneness in facing the world that makes roses so unlikely.

At the same time we know that the absence, for all its dread, is not new. Our people have seen this before. It is recorded in our ancient stories. It's no use to be condemning the modern world. No use launching into a diatribe against technology or an indictment of consumer culture or a tirade against Sunday shopping. The absence of God is not caused by those things. The absence of God is as old as the hills. Older. The Book of Job knows all about it:

> Oh that I knew where I might find him ...
> Behold I go forward but he is not there;
> And backward, but I cannot perceive him;
> On the left hand I seek him but I cannot behold him;
> I turn to the right hand, but I cannot see him ...
> For I am hemmed in by darkness,
> And thick darkness covers my face. (Job 23:3ff)

Job—now there's a human being with problems. His
health is rocky. He's got business failure. He's got family
dynamics—what's left of his family. He's got emotional issues.
But his biggest problem, the one he rails and rages and rebels
against, is the absence. The godless, inscrutable absence.

I called you—no reply.
I was faithful—no reward.
I prayed—you hid your face.
I turned to the right and to the left—you just left.

Job is a decent human being but he is living in an absence,
thick darkness upon his face. Millions of us decent human
beings live in an absence. It's especially poignant for minis-
ters, who have to keep talking as if God is here, all the while
wondering how many people notice the thick darkness upon
our faces.

Yet through all this, Job is discovering something about
the living God. In the awful absence, Job has come face to face
with the wildness of God.

That may be an odd way to say this—that God is wild.
Theologians might use different language. They might say that
God is sovereign. Or that God is inscrutable. Or that God is
free. But I am saying that God is wild because that is the only
clear way to convey that God is not domestic.

We call creatures "wild" when their ways are not our
ways. They have their own ways. The ways of the wild are not
arbitrary or random or chaotic. They are not in contravention
of all law. The wild ones have their own mysterious laws. They
follow their own deep rhythms and patterns. They move to
the sound of a music we cannot hear. Weather is wild in this
sense, too. The wind blows where it wills. Thus it is with the
Spirit: like the wind, said Jesus, wild like the wind.

The Book of Job is all about God who has never been
tamed and who does not show up when summoned. It is all

about, "Where is God when you need him?" About a good
man who calls God to his side in a time of trial and is met
with silence.

It's a terrible thing. I know a lot of people who, because
of it, have abandoned faith. They've turned out the lights
inside, locked the door, and walked out alone into the night.
They discard the Bible and its wild stories. They say it isn't
truc.

The truth is, the Bible knows all about the absence of
God. The Bible knows that God cannot be captured and
trained. It knows that God is not, in this sense, available.

God says:
"You cannot see my face …"
"My ways are not your ways …"
"I am who I am and I will be what I am doing …"

In the book of Ezekiel, the presence of God is described
as a glory or a radiant effulgence. The rabbinic word for this
effulgence is *shekinah*. According to Ezekiel, the glory or the
*shekinah* one day escapes out of the temple. Glory escapes
and moves out over the city, over the wall, down through
a ravine, and out into the hills. It disappears. It is last seen
heading east. Some presume it has gone all the way across
the desert to Babylon. Imagine *that*, for a moment, if you
were a loyal Israelite. Imagine the glory taking up with the
Babylonians!

"I will be who I will be," says the Lord. "And I will go
where I will go and I will hang with whom I will hang."

God will not be defined by Israel's religion. It's in the
Bible. God will not be confined by Israel's nationalism. It's in
the Bible. God will not be tamed by any religious tradition, no
matter how loudly and how long that tradition booms out the
divine name.

So if you feel that God is far away, you might be right. The glory might have slipped away while you were tending to the accoutrements of the temple. It has happened before. We are, most of the time, children of a dreadful absence. We are citizens of the wild kingdom, a kingdom we may belong to but which never belongs to us.

We cannot change any of this. But here are three things I think a person can do.

First, find a place in the church. Even if you are a mouse in the corner, find someplace where you can overhear the stories, especially the unlikely ones, the unmanageable ones, the untamed ones. They are most like God.

We don't go to church because God is present there. We go to church because in most of our experience, most of the time, God is absent. Oh, there is the rare and stunning moment of God's appearing in the landscape of a day, but it is a brief and passing moment. Most of our time is spent in the absence.

People think we're stupid to go to church. They say, "You're not aflame with faith and free. You're just going there out of habit: Sunday morning, sun comes up, having no will and no freedom of your own, you trudge off to church just like always."

Well, we're not that stupid. We are in the church because the community holds the faith and tells it and sings it when we cannot hold it and tell it and sing it for ourselves. The community remembers when we have forgotten. The community speaks the sacred name even when it has fallen silent on our lips. The community knows it's God's world even when we've become convinced that the world is a godforsaken wilderness of abandoned dreams and broken promises.

So find your place in the church where the tales of the wild God are remembered and told: God in the rain ... God in a pregnancy ... God in an execution ... Find a place in the church where the powerful hope is proclaimed that God shall come again, like a shoot from a great tree cut down, or like a rose blooming amid the cold of winter.

The second thing you can do is stop worrying about being well-adjusted. Beware the therapists who counsel adjustment to a godforsaken world. Job never accepted the absence. He railed, he raged, he rebelled. He refused the therapies offered to him. He would settle for no domestic imitation and neither must you. If you are not angry in a godforsaken world there's something wrong. You've achieved adjustment. You've imbibed the indifference that promotes itself as open-mindedness. You've come to tolerate everything—even the intolerable.

Canada may be a proud jurisdiction, but it has an intolerable rate of violence against gay and lesbian people. Canadian politicians may be fond of saying that Canada is the best country in the world, but the casinos are full and the churches are empty. Canada may be prosperous according to the national fiscal forecast, but it doesn't apply to any First Nations reserve I've ever been on. Don't adjust to these things. God may not be available but God is still God. When we shake a fist at the sky and shout, "God, where are you? How could you let this happen?" we are likely to hear the reply, "Indeed, where are you? How could *you?*"

Besides, remember Ezekiel and the glory? One day, it returned. Not that anyone was holding out much hope. After all, the glory had been gone for nineteen years. People had grown accustomed to its absence. People had adjusted. But one day, out of nowhere, there it was, coming over the hills, headed for the temple.

How long has the glory been gone where you live? Days? Months? Years? Have you adjusted to the absence? Have you found stand-ins for the glory in the calculations of a successful life? Have you found substitutes for the glory in the techniques of a successful church? If you ever adjust to its being gone you won't have found reality, you'll have lost the wild gift of hope.

So be alert. You never know when the *shekinah* will be coming over the horizon—like a thief in the night, as Jesus said (1 Thessalonians 5:2).

The third thing you can do is plant your young apple trees. This is what Martin Luther said he'd be doing if he knew it was his last day in the world—he'd be out planting life, planting young apple trees. Let God find you alive and at work, nurturing life when God chooses the time of appearing.

This is why God has given you moments to remember, when the glory drew near and you took off your shoes. So that you would know the way of life until God shall come again, like the rain, in God's own sweet time. Ethics is what we do while God is away.

But mark this. One day God will appear. Like that ragged figure Flannery O'Connor describes, the one that moves from tree to tree in the back of the mind. Or like the glory appearing over a distant hill. Or like a morsel of bread dipped in a cup. Or like a rose blooming amid the cold of winter when half-spent is the night.

Then you will know why you kept the faith—or more truthfully, why the faith kept you. On that day when the wild and holy one appears you can say, "Glory, I've been watching for you and waiting. I've been hoping you'd come. Roses are difficult here."

------

Peter Short is a minister of the United Church of Canada and author of *Outside Eden: Essays of Encouragement*. He has been in church ministry since 1977, serving churches on Quebec's Gaspé Coast, in Yellowknife and Montreal, and currently in Fredericton, New Brunswick. He was moderator of the denomination from 2003 to 2006, when his articles in the *United Church Observer* won reader acclaim and church press awards.

Leaps of Faith

# On Pioneering
*~ Marie-Louise Ternier-Gommers ~*

*Now the LORD said to Abram, "Go from your country and your kindred and*
*your father's house to the land that I will show you ... and I will bless you."*
(Genesis 12:1–3)

*Do not follow where the path may lead.*
*Go instead where there is no path and leave a trail.*
(Harold R. McAlindon)

One day my book editor told me that I'm affectionately called the
"Hyphenated One" at his office. I sighed. Even after living in Canada
for nearly thirty years, I still have to fight to keep my long name. I
had a medical appointment recently. "Marie Ternier, please," the receptionist called out in the waiting area. I didn't recognize my name,
and she called a second time. "Marie Ternier, please."

I got up. "The name is Marie-Louise, with a hyphen," I said,
"and Ternier-Gommers, with another hyphen. Computers hate
my name, but truly, I'm never called Marie." The receptionist
barely took note of my speech.

I went home and mused. *What's next?* I wondered. Thoughts
of a life spent pioneering bubbled up ...

Getting married is a major move in anyone's life, but I com-
pounded the matter by marrying a man from far, far away, from a
place no one knew. "What in the world has she found in Canada,
so far away from everywhere?" friends and family were thinking
when I returned home to the Netherlands with an engagement
ring on my finger. They were thinking "immigrants, pioneering,
adventure." I assured folks that the country was by now well-
developed and quite with the times—by no means as rugged as
some Dutch settlers had found it decades earlier. The pioneering
was done, I said, and I would simply reap the fruits of the sweat
and blood those settlers had shed to open up the West.

They might have believed me had I not shown them a photograph of a house—on a truck—and announced I was going to live there. A house on a truck being moved some twenty-five kilometres to be plunked on the slope of a small hill in the Saskatchewan Parklands, at the end of a gravel road, by a lake. By Dutch standards this was synonymous with "the boonies" and meant to my mother that the earth was indeed flat as a pancake and that her daughter was about to perch on its very edge—the end of the world.

In marrying Jim, I also married a country, a culture, and a lifestyle. But the excitement of new beginnings was electric. We were going to make a difference in the world—as a married couple, as Catholic Christians, as Saskatchewan farmers. We were not comfortable with adopting unquestioned middle-class, materialistic values, nor did we think of farming as agribusiness. The rebel in us pushed us into countercultural choices.

This was pioneering in reverse: from a consumer lifestyle with all conveniences back to a life of voluntary simplicity, the basics. The prison of modern living looked more suffocating to us than the time-consuming and labour-intensive activities of hauling water from the lake, growing and preserving our own food, and chopping wood for cooking and heating. William McNamara's spirituality, as described in the book *Mystical Passion*, became real for us:

> I share the secret of the child, of the saints and sages, as well as of clowns and fools when I realize how wondrous and marvelous it is to carry fuel and draw water. Once the spiritual significance of such ordinary earthy acts dawns on me, I can skip the yoga and koans, the mantras and novenas.

We gardened organically and sold vegetables at the local farmers' market. This focus eventually shifted into growing organic garden seeds for sale. I learned all about preserving

our winter's supply of food and baking bread using the wood
stove—things that were not part of my upbringing. We even used
a natural method of family planning by observing body symp-
toms and charting body temperature.

For nearly twenty years we lived close to the earth and in
harmony with the rhythms of nature. At nineteen, our daughter
wrote to us about her gratitude to "non-materialistic, simple living, happy, grateful, and generous parents" and went on to list all
the values she had learnt in her growing-up years. Not bad for a
pair of idealistic hippies!

My parents' goal in life had been to get away from the
"deprived" life in order to offer the next generation more material comfort and affluence. One becomes a "pioneer" in order
to improve one's material lot in life, not to reverse it, or so the
popular understanding implies. And so my parents never understood the strange kind of freedom and independence that comes
with freely choosing a simple back-to-the-land existence.

Pioneering at its core is really about that—discovering a new
way not as an end in itself, but in order to live in freedom, physically, mentally, socially, and spiritually. Cultural and social confor-
mity is the antithesis of pioneering. That is why so many who are
considered pioneers are individuals who step outside the norm,
who don't fit in any box, whose vision is larger and wider than
what presents itself as the horizon, whose faith in a bigger picture
leaves them so restless that they have to step off the beaten track.

I stepped off the beaten track all right, in more ways than
one, the day I married. Now, twenty-eight years later, I see a
path marked by both blessing and pain. Taking charge of our
own health through choices in lifestyle and working the land
paid off in more ways than economic. What a rich feeling when
freezer and sealers were full of home-grown food and when one
hundred dollars lasted longer than a week! Our choice in family
planning was in sync with the rest of our lives and we had three
lovely children.

Despite our attempts to live a "pioneering" life in response
to the gospel call to live fully, we were perceived as odd. Within
our rural prairie Catholic parish we were considered lopsided
hippies—back-to-the-landers who attend church? Local "real"
back-to-the-landers viewed us with suspicion; we had not, after all,
turned our back on all of society nor on the institutional church.
Again, I wondered: what is pioneering and who defines it?

As our children grew older, I became interested in going
to school. Pioneering of a very different sort beckoned: good
Catholic girl off to university—a Lutheran seminary to be
precise—at age thirty-five while raising three children and living a two-hour commute away. Spurred on by a desire to obtain
more knowledge and training in pastoral counselling, I devoured
theology, liturgy, and church history courses. The hunger to learn
about the things of God had lain dormant for several decades.
Walking into these classes on theology, liturgy, and spirituality
reawakened the old flame. It felt new, exciting and ... familiar.
Little did I know that another unexpected turn in the road would
lead into further uncharted territory.

It was a course on preaching that held the pioneering
surprise. I was reluctant and impatient at first, not seeing new
potential at all. I even felt slightly annoyed that such a class was
required for my degree. Just as Sarah did when overhearing
strangers say she would have a son in her old age (Genesis 18:9–
12), I laughed in secret at the absurdity of the situation. Here
I was, a Roman Catholic woman, learning from the Lutherans
how to preach God's Word in the pulpit! I thought the combination ludicrous. I would probably not learn very much, let alone
ever use what I'd learned. To top off the situation's absurdity, the
professor was an ordained Lutheran woman, the first ordained
woman I'd ever faced in a close encounter.

But a pioneer has her heart always open to new possibilities,
however absurd they may seem at first. And so, crazy as it felt, the
question whether I had a call to preach began to surface. I was raised

in a church tradition where there was no expectation, let alone possibility, that preaching could be part of my ministry. Until this class, the Catholic climate had kept such a question safely at bay.

I discovered that church structures greatly affect our experience of God's call and our ability to respond to that call. If church structures do not permit the experience of being called by God either to preaching and/or ordination, and do not permit the discernment and response to such a call, then such questions may not necessarily surface directly in a person's consciousness. For the first time ever, I started wondering if this is what happens when a Roman Catholic woman dares to claim being called by God to preach and/or to ordained ministry. Once again, the notion of "pioneering" was slowly being written all over this alluring journey.

Now an ecclesial pioneer, my voice was changing and my heart began to hear new songs. I was desperately looking for new ways to "sing," even though I remained uncertain about how, where, and when to sing. Does a real pioneer always know exactly what lies beyond the horizon? One of our textbooks, *A Little Exercise for Young Theologians* by Helmut Thielicke, proved immeasurably helpful: "During the period when the voice is changing we do not sing, and during this formative period in the life of the theological student he [she] does not preach." These words gave me permission to let the process take its course without the pressure of needing to share answers I did not yet have. For now, remaining faithfully rooted in God and prayerfully alert to the inner movements was sufficient. I prayed and learned, learned and prayed, continuously offering to God the deep stirrings of my heart.

After graduation, I worked as editor for a Canadian Catholic family magazine. At the same time, and much to my own surprise, I quickly became the local supply preacher-in-residence for the Anglicans, the Lutherans, the United Church folks, the Presbyterians, and even for the Mennonites and the Worldwide

Church of God. An even greater surprise awaited me when the pulpit in my own Catholic parish opened up when we conducted our own Sunday Service of the Word with communion. (Our priest had six parishes!) My preaching became a vehicle for ecumenical ministry and offered a glimpse of increasing lay involvement in pastoral and liturgical leadership, both unprecedented in my neck of the woods. Forging a way to this through preaching—how brilliant, God, I thought; I couldn't have come up with a better plan.

Despite all the affirmations, however, I remained uncomfortable with the position I occupied in the local Christian family. I indeed felt like a pioneer, like I did when I moved to this vast country from the tiny, crowded Low Countries. There was, however, a big difference between the adventuresome spirit that characterized that move and my mid-life need for stability and predictability. The pioneer in me was now at odds with the part in me that strongly needed to simply belong in one place, one "box," one church family. As a young adult, life was filled with making new choices and exploring new territory. Now I just wanted to slow down and continue on well-chosen paths. But nothing seemed further from reality. The road, in fact, was to be created, not followed.

One of the hardest parts was to allow God's Spirit to redefine where, and to whom, I belonged in relationship to God, others, myself, the church. My formation in ministry and church leadership resulted in a changed relationship with both clergy and laity; I belonged to both groups and to neither at the same time. Moreover, I felt forced to shed the false security of thinking that the direction of my life even remotely "belonged" to me anyway.

I appreciated anew Jesus' words in response to one enthusiastic follower who said, "I will follow you wherever you go." Jesus said to him, "Foxes have holes, and birds of the air have nests; but the Son of Man has nowhere to lay his head" (Luke

9:57–58). In some ways, I belonged everywhere and nowhere.
I belonged in my Roman Catholic tradition, yet moved freely in
other sanctuaries. I belonged with the laity, for that is what I was
in my own tradition. Yet in some ways I also belonged with the
clergy because of a formation that profoundly changed my self-
identity, a change that our tradition calls an "indelible mark on
the soul." Pioneers belong everywhere and nowhere; they belong
to Life itself.

And so, unlike what I tried to tell my family and friends
back in the Netherlands when I moved to Canada, the pioneering was not done. It never is. For a big part of pioneering is to
be radically open to new possibilities, open to surprises, open to
grace in unexpected places. It's about knowing that the horizon
is merely an optical illusion, that there is a greater world, a wider
vision, which beckons us always to step off the beaten track and
to live life following in God's footprint, with *only* God's footprint
to guide us.

"Take nothing for your journey, no staff, nor bag, nor bread,
nor money—not even an extra tunic," Jesus said (Luke 9:3).
And, "Whatever town or village you enter, find out who in it is
worthy, and stay there until you leave" (Matthew 10:11).

---

Marie-Louise Ternier-Gommers, MTS, is the author of two
books published by Novalis. Her first book, *Finding the
Treasure Within; A Woman's Journey into Preaching*, won a Catholic
Press Association award in 2003. She has preached and been
retreat facilitator in various Christian denominations, is writing
and editing for two religious orders, and is now employed in pastoral ministry at her local Catholic parish. Mother of three adult
children, she and her husband Jim live in Humboldt,
Saskatchewan.

# Surprised by Goodness
(for June Callwood*, gratefully)
~ *Mary Jo Leddy* ~

"So do you think we can count on goodness?" She leaned across the table, asking as if our lives depended on the answer. That was during my first Monday lunch with June Callwood more than twenty-five years ago. I knew then that she had understood something foundational was at stake, a determination that could make all the difference in the world. We were each, in different ways, thinking long and hard about whether we could count on goodness and kindness to change the world. That question would be the underlying theme of our monthly luncheons over the many years to come.

June came to her own hard-won answers over those years. In some ways it was easier for me, not so much because of what I believed but because of where I lived. It is not that I see more clearly than June, but I do see reality more surely—perhaps because I have had the privilege of living and working with refugees for the past sixteen years.

I never intended to get involved with refugees. Seventeen years ago there were other "causes" and "issues" I was more concerned about. It really was by the way, by accident as it were, that I met a refugee woman from Eritrea and her five children. It was the moment when I was faced, summoned, commanded. I recall that moment, one now repeated many times over in various and different ways.

> *There is a knock at the door.*
> *You can choose not to answer.*
> *For reasons unclear even to yourself*
> *you open the door slightly and see*

---

*June Rose Callwood was a Toronto journalist, author, and social activist who died in April 2007.

*THE EYES and then*
*the blur of a face as it looks down*
*and then up again.*
*It is the face of a stranger,*
*the face of a woman.*
*You do not know who she is;*
*you do not even know who you are, for sure.*
*You could close the door. Perhaps she senses this.*
*The face of the woman with the eyes*
*says what she cannot speak:*
*"You must help me."*
*You could say no.*
*You do not know what to do.*
*You used to know before*
*you learned how systems can file*
*people away—forever.*
*But you know you are, here and now*
*the one, the one who must respond:*
*This YOU must do. There is no other.*
*You are faced.*
*The stranger moves forward*
*and fills the frame of your mind*
*and slowly comes into focus.*
*and you become focused.*
*Your life becomes weighty, consequential, significant.*

It is this face-to-face encounter, more than any sense of guilt or righteousness, that becomes the core of the ethical experience that has guided my work for justice. Such a moment evokes feelings of compassion which lead to practical forms of kindness. It is within this reach of mercy that I have become convinced of the necessity—and near impossibility—of justice.

You see there is a person and so you see there is a problem. You have been faced by someone and you begin to see that the systems they are forced to live in seem designed to deface human beings, to render them invisible, to muffle their cry for justice and their hope for peace. This is a social and even spiritual shock for the one who now knows the refugee by name, who sees the face as the landscape of one particular history. This person has been given a Client ID number and has been filed away in the nice Canadian way. From time to time pro forma letters arrive to signal that another hurdle has been passed and that the end, the place of safety, has been reached.

However, sometimes the letter says, "You have not been determined to be a Convention Refugee." And then, "You have fifteen days to present yourself at the Immigration Detention Centre." Case closed. Another life is filed away.

The immigration officer who issued the form letter never has to see the hand that trembles after the envelope is opened. If you are near, not far away in some clinical distance or protected by the illusion of social objectivity, you tremble and are afraid.

This is the time of temptation. It is all too easy to begin to demonize particular people who are supposedly in charge of the system that churns out such cruelty. It is tempting to caricature the struggle as that of *us* against *them*. Indeed, such a take on the way things work tends to attract people inclined to this dualistic way of looking at the world. *We* are right and *they* are wrong. *We* are on the side of the angels against the demonic forces of evil.

The struggle is to remain life-size in a time of hyper-morality. The refugee advocate, who now knows the real refugee, who is neither better nor worse than the conventional stereotype, must resist the temptation to demonize immigration officials and politicians. It is a challenge to continue to believe that the employees of the system are also human and could be summoned to life-size responsibility.

Hannah Arendt observed that in some medieval paintings, the devil is depicted as the faceless one, the masked one, the nobody. In the various systems that hold the power of life and death over refugees, it often seems that nobody is responsible. Some refugees who arrive in Canada learn what happens when nobody is responsible. Nobody can kill you, just as anybody or somebody could do so.

One of the challenges of working with refugees, with people who are poor, with those who have been violated, is to summon all concerned to face themselves. It becomes an ethical impera-tive to say: "Systems have been created by human beings and therefore can be changed by human beings; systems must be changed so that human beings can face each other and face the consequences of their actions."

I once witnessed an interview between an immigration of-ficer and a widow from Africa who had arrived in Canada with her two little boys. The officer began by asking the standard ques-tions about why she was afraid for her safety and that of her sons. After he had made some sketchy notes, he looked up and asked, rather sarcastically, "So what do you think you have to contribute to this country?" She thought for a while and then said, quite simply, "My children. I contribute my children."

"Yeah sure," he said. He left the room and then we did. As we were going down the corridor toward the exit, I caught sight of him turning a corner and went after him in a fury. "She was right, you know. And don't you know? If someone asked you what might be the most important thing you would contribute with your life, wouldn't you say your children?" He blushed, looked down, and walked away.

We need to remain life-size in a time of hypermorality when we cast for angels and demons in political dramas. We tend to demonize our opponents and can see no good in them. We may think we have to idealize the causes we work for, all the while knowing the struggles, the uncertainties, and the frailties of the people we count on as allies.

To remain life-size involves reclaiming the ordinary, daily quality of evil. Most of the evil in this world is not done by vicious monsters but by people who are thoughtless, who turn away, who shrug off responsibility, who are simply too busy to care. This is what Hannah Arendt called the banality of evil—and it is sadly predictable. However, if we take this ordinary evil for granted, the systems of injustice will grind on. Evil may be predictable but it is neither inevitable nor invincible.

Resisting the banality of evil involves, I believe, a spirited and stubborn refusal to take ordinary goodness for granted.

Night after night, in Toronto where I live, a young man by the name of Jecob Myoboke goes to the Air Canada Centre to work for minimum wage. He rolls up the turf after sports events and puts away the floors after rock concerts. As the sun begins to rise, he goes home and sleeps for three hours before he goes on to his next job at a garage. He has arranged his work so that he can be home in time to cook supper for his younger brother, Abel. This way, he can be sure Abel does his homework and says his prayers at night. Abel is a soccer star, someone who dances with the stars and hopes to go to university.

Jecob and Abel came to Romero House from Rwanda after they had been orphaned during the genocide. Jecob was fifteen and Abel was twelve. They do not know who brought them to Canada or why. They huddled together in the bus terminal on Bay Street for two days until someone from Africa spoke to them in their own language and then phoned Romero House. Jecob has been working since he was fifteen to support his little brother.

It is such as he, it is such daily goodness, that upholds this city.

On the street where I live there is a mother who keeps herself awake at night by making lovely cards with dried flowers, who keeps herself awake so she can be attentive to the breathing of her severely disabled son. It is people such as she who sustain our neighbourhood. It is people such as the hundreds, the thousands, of mothers and fathers who awaken every

night to the sound of their child crying, and who stay awake
until the child settles. And who go to work tired and who are
ready to wake up in the middle of the night again and again.
This is the ordinary goodness and generosity that sustains the
fabric of our society.

North of this city, in a remote and vast area called the Con-
roy Marsh, a monk chants in the forest although hardly anyone
hears. A few years ago, a friend and I discovered his one-room
log "monastery" when we had lost our way while looking for a
camping spot. The monk lives on berries, vegetables, and fish.
His life has become a praiseworthy chant. It is such as these who
sustain the universe.

This is ordinary goodness and we are surrounded and upheld
by it everyday. It should never be taken for granted. We need to
take note of goodness.

You and I have a very fundamental choice to make. We must
decide whether we are going to believe that people tend toward
goodness or tend toward evil. This is not only a philosophical or
theological question but also a matter of great personal and political importance. How we weigh in on this question will make
a great difference in our lives and in the world in which we live
and move and have our being. The evidence before us is inconclu-
sive. The earth holds the memory of genocide and environmental
degradation; it also preserves the relics of great beauty and social
conservation. In the end, how we weigh in on the world with our
lives becomes something like an act of faith.

When we sift and sort our own lives do we expect that we
are better than we know or worse than we think? When we lobby
for social change are we going to expect people to do the right
thing or will we expect indifference and hostility?

The astonishing reality is that our belief in the basic tenden-
cy of human beings will become a self-fulfilling prophecy.

If we expect the best in others, and in ourselves, we will
sometimes be disappointed but we will, more often than not,

find the good that we are looking for. If we expect the worst in others, and in ourselves, we will probably find it.

Nevertheless, I believe that the future will belong to politicians and public figures who summon what is best in us and what is good in this country—who remind us that we can act out of great decency and generosity, that we are capable of caring about more than ourselves, capable of investing in a future that we might never see, capable of loving this fragile and astonishing country called Canada, capable of caring about the earth as our common good.

As I have reflected on the enormous outpouring of gratitude for the life of June Callwood, I have come to think that people were touched by her faith in what was best in us. She did not come to this belief easily or lightly—she was too intelligent and perceptive for that. Nevertheless, she weighed in with her life and chose to give more weight to goodness and kindness.

It is easy and tempting to define ourselves in terms of who or what we are against. The rest of the country may define itself by being against Toronto, or we may all define Canada by being against the United States. Socially conscious people may define themselves by being against injustice, against racism, against violence. The tragic reality is that we will inevitably become like that which we are fighting against. In long struggle against injustice, racism, and violence, we will become unjust, racist, and violent. It makes all the difference in the world whether we are *for* justice or *against* injustice. If you look at injustice long enough it goes through your eyes to the back of your head and you begin to replicate the patterns of thought that you have become all too familiar with.

To return to the experience of seeing a problem when you have first seen a person—this person is not an abstraction, a cause, an issue, an object of social concern. This person has a name and a face and, in time, you will have a great affection for her and her children, and for the husband and father who finally arrives. This is who you are for. This is why you can think with affection and act with affection. The struggle and failure will continue, social analysis and strategizing will become even more imperative, and the meetings will still be boring and interminable.

Nevertheless, you will know who you are for and why you are acting for social justice. Then it gets a little easier to begin to think about how to effect change. For sure, this I know for sure.

---

Mary Jo Leddy is a writer and activist. She was the founding editor of the independent national newspaper *Catholic New Times* and is the author of hundreds of articles on social and religious themes. She has also written seven books, including the best-selling *Radical Gratitude*. In 1997 she received the Order of Canada. For the last eighteen years she has lived and worked with refugees at the Romero House Community in Toronto.

# Crossing to the Other Side
~ *James Loney* ~

*It takes a long time not to feel like an alien, a long time to feel at home,*
*a long time to search out and discover who you are. But if you go all*
*the way with that exploration, it takes you beyond race, beyond colour,*
*beyond class, beyond every kind of category, and you find that you belong*
*to humanity. And that's who you are ... and when you are that, there is*
*no foreign land.Wherever you are is home. And the earth is paradise and*
*wherever you set your feet is holy land.*

—Wilfred Peltier, Anishinabe elder, from *No Foreign Land*

I want to tell you about the first time I went to the other side.
It was in May of 1987 and I was twenty-two years old. I had
been accepted as a volunteer with the Via Veritas program run
by Virginia Nelson, a sister of St. Joseph in Toronto. This program placed volunteers in native communities where there was
a Catholic mission. Filled with idealistic zeal, I wanted to make
a difference in the world. I wanted to help people. I wanted to
live with the poor and learn from them. I had recently learned
about the miserable social conditions that First Nations people
in Canada were subject to (and still are), and this seemed like a
good way for me to begin.

Sister Virginia told me, "I think God is calling you to leave
everything behind and to enter a new land—just like Abraham."
So she sent me to God's Lake Narrows, a Cree community of
1,200 in northern Manitoba that you can only reach by flying.
When I got to Winnipeg, I had to leave the main airport terminal to find the secondary terminal where I could catch my final
plane. I stepped into a cramped, wood-frame building lined with
indestructible plastic seats—nothing like the shiny, airy,
important-looking architecture I'd just come from.

I looked at all the faces of the people waiting and was instantly afraid. I felt I had entered another world. I was the only
one in the room with white skin, except for those working

behind the baggage counter. I became conscious, for the first time in my life, that I had a skin colour and that the colour of my skin meant something. I imagined that everyone was scrutinizing me, wondering who I was and what my purpose was.

I was afraid because I felt so different, and I was upset with my obsessive awareness of being different. I thought I had successfully trained myself to be comfortable with racial and cultural differences—an easy thing to do as long as I enjoyed the safety of belonging to the majority. But now that the tables were turned, now that I was the outsider, I was forced to confront an uneasy truth about myself: despite my illusions to the contrary, I too was bound by racialized categories of *us* and *them*.

An Oblate brother named Thomas Novak met me at the airstrip in God's Lake Narrows. He was not the kind of missionary who seeks out converts. In many ways he was trying to repair the harm that had been done under that old understanding of mission. His goal was to be a presence of solidarity and friendship, to help God's Lake Catholics live out their faith in the context of their own history and culture.

Those first few days were excruciating. Whenever I get really stressed I get cramps, and the only thing that eases them is lying down. I had cramps all the time, so I hid in my room as much as I could. When people came by the mission house to visit Thomas, I would get up and join them in a stark, wood-panelled living room furnished with those plywood and metal tube chairs from the 1960s. I would sit there and wrack my brain for something to say. Most of the time I couldn't say anything at all. I was afraid of saying something culturally inappropriate, of being judged or rejected, afraid because I didn't belong and didn't know how to belong.

But I had come to volunteer and I was determined to make myself useful. That is, after all, white-middle-class rule number one: when in doubt, make yourself useful. I asked Thomas if I could paint the mission house. It was in desperate need of painting and I figured that would be a good place to start in terms of being useful. Thomas got me some tools and a homemade scaffold and I got to work.

There were always kids hanging out at the mission house. I liked that because at that time, when I was so shy and afraid of who I was, kids were really the only people in whose presence I felt I could be myself. I had worked seven summers at a camp for boys from poor families.

It was a beautiful June day, warm enough to take my shirt off, and I managed somehow to forget myself in the vigour of feeling useful, the sounds of God's Lake lapping against its round granite shores, the wind whispering its way through scraggly black spruce spires. That is, until one of the kids who lived nearby came around. His name was Jack. He was seventeen, a lot bigger than me, and he had a soccer ball. He shyly asked if I would play with him. I was immediately filled with dread. I was hopelessly incompetent at sports and couldn't kick a soccer ball to save my life. Somehow I managed to say yes. (I didn't figure out until later that he was developmentally disabled.)

I was almost crippled with self-consciousness as I ran after the soccer ball in my clumsy way. A voice in my head kept saying Jack must be collecting scornful epithets about my lack of skill to trade with his buddies later on. But then I began to see that Jack couldn't care less about my soccer abilities. He was smiling and laughing, totally immersed in the pleasures of kicking a soccer ball around and happy just to have someone to play with.

Others joined in and soon a spontaneous community pick-up soccer game was in full swing, with six-year-olds and teenagers and adults all playing together. I suddenly discovered myself full of joy, my sense of being separate dissolved in the camaraderie and out-of-breath laughter of human beings at play. People shouted and joked in Cree. There wasn't much I could understand, but I felt I completely belonged. My fear disappeared.

One of my favourite stories in the Christian Scriptures expresses well what happened to me during that sojourn at God's
Lake Narrows.

> On that day, when evening had come, [Jesus] said to [his
> disciples], "Let us go across to the other side." And leaving
> the crowd behind, they took him with them in the boat, just
> as he was. Other boats were with him. A great windstorm
> arose, and the waves beat into the boat, so that the boat
> was already being swamped. But he was in the stern, asleep
> on the cushion; and they woke him up and said to him,
> "Teacher, do you not care that we are perishing?" He woke
> up and rebuked the wind, and said to the sea, "Peace! Be
> still!" Then the wind ceased, and there was a dead calm. He
> said to them, "Why are you afraid? Have you still no faith?"
> And they were filled with great awe and said to one another,
> "Who then is this, that even the wind and the sea obey him?"
> (Mark 4:35–41)

I used to think this story was mainly about having faith that
Jesus is always with us in the storms of life and therefore we
don't need to be afraid. But when I learned what that curious
little phrase "the other side" meant, I began to see a whole other
dimension to the story. "The other side" symbolizes the land that
is outside and beyond "Israel"—beyond the place where people
speak the same language, pray to the same God, live according to
the same rules, and see themselves as belonging together. For us,
Israel can be a country, an ethnicity, a gender or sexual orientation, a skin colour, a religion—even a bowling team—anything
that involves a strongly defined sense of *we* that sets us apart in an
enclosure of safety and belonging.

Across from Israel lies the land of the other, the one who is
not like me, who looks and smells and dresses differently, follows different rules, believes different things, wears strange hats,

and worships strange gods in strange ways. The other side is the
world of the stranger, the one who does not belong, the one who
confounds and contradicts the *we* that I belong to and feel safe in.
The other is either someone I must approach with caution, or a
threat that must be destroyed.

Jesus says, "Let us go over to the other side." Go to the
strange world of the stranger. Go to the place where you are a
foreigner among foreigners. Go outside the land where your
language, your ways of knowing and understanding and relating don't work and everything is confusing. Go where you will
be totally helpless and depend on the hospitality of those you've
been taught to fear and despise.

Anyone who's journeyed outside their own culture and
language knows very well the disorientation and vulnerability
that result when we find ourselves in the foreign land of the
other side. The term often used to describe this unravelling of
our identity is *culture shock*. I remember spending the summer of
1992 in Mexico and feeling this profound sense of inner poverty
and worthlessness. Unable to speak Spanish, I couldn't commu-
nicate anything of who I was: my ideas, where I was from, what
I did in Canada. I barely knew enough Spanish to ask where the
bathroom was. I felt like a child.

So Jesus and the disciples get into a boat and journey to the other
side. The little vessel they travel in represents the ego, the self, all
the mental and emotional constructions we think make up who we
are. And what happens to that identity when we journey to the other
side and are confronted by the other—the one-who-is-not-like-us, the
one who breaks our rules that govern what it means to be a person?
We are forced to rethink who we are and what land we belong to.

In crossing to the other side of God's Lake Narrows, I was
forced to become conscious of the fact that I was naturally comfortable with people who had the same skin colour as me, and
conversely afraid of those whose skin colour was different. In my
encounter with the Cree of Manitoba, I had to confront the ugly

fact that racism was an integral part of my identity. I thought white (or more accurately, pink) skin was normal and safe, and that other skin colours were not.

The fear and anguish I felt in those first days at God's Lake were the furious squall we see in Mark's story. My little boat, my sense of who I was, was being swamped. Some part of who I *thought* I was was changing, dying. That's what happens to us in a cross cultural experience, in the encounter with the other. Some part of us dies. We no longer understand who we are or where we fit, and we start to panic for fear of disappearing under the waves altogether.

This leads to that little phrase that is so easy to miss: "Leaving the crowd behind, they took Jesus along, *just as he was*, into the boat." They took him along, *just as he was*. It strikes me that Jesus is the true self within the boat, the true self that's eternally and irrevocably alive within us. But my true self had fallen asleep on a little cushion—the comfort and predict-ability of my own private "Israel" that I unconsciously relied on for my sense of safety and belonging. The storm we encounter as we leave that land and cross to the other side awakens the true self and reveals that what the false self had taken to be solid ground, a place to stand and to be someone—is really an illusion. The false self finds itself perilously awash, stranded without a rudder, sinking under the waves. The disciples say, "Teacher, do you not care that we are perishing?" Something of the false self does in fact die in the encounter with the other, and something of the true self awakens.

What dies in the encounter with the other is the sense of separateness we construct from the raw material of our society, our culture, our language, our bodies, our thoughts, our experi-ences, our feelings, how people see us, how we see the world. The false self is made up of all the thoughts and feelings and identities that set us apart from everyone and everything else. And sin, if we remember our theology, is anything that separates us from God and from each other.

The true self is not separate or apart. It is a reality, a mystery that is beyond observation, language, biography—every kind of category, in fact—and exists in active, continuous, irrevocable communion with God. Thomas Merton describes the true self this way: "At the centre of our being is a point of nothingness which is untouched by sin and illusion, a point of pure truth ... a point or spark, which belongs entirely to God ... this little point is the pure glory of God in us ... it is like a pure diamond, blazing with the invisible light of heaven. It is in everybody."

As I look back, the fear I experienced when I left the crowd behind and stepped into that airport terminal to go to God's Lake was a sign to me. It was the furious squall telling me, "Wake up. The false self is in charge and it doesn't know where it's going." That fear was telling me that my identity had been colonized by something false, something wrong: a racial hierarchy that was separating me from those who did not have pink skin. And it was through my encounter with the other, the one I was so afraid of, that I caught my first glimpse of that little spark of the invisible light of heaven in me, and in everyone around me, and took my first steps into Abraham's new land where everyone belongs and no one need be afraid.

I went to God's Lake Narrows thinking I was going to help impoverished native people, but instead I received an extraordinary gift. I began to feel I could really belong to the human race. I learned there is no foreign land, everywhere is home, and everyone is a brother or sister created by God to laugh and play together in a great cosmic game of soccer, and the only rule is an invitation: come and be yourself.

---

James Loney is a reservist with Christian Peacemaker Teams (CPT). He was part of a CPT delegation that was kidnapped in Baghdad in November 2006 and held hostage for four months.

James has also served on CPT projects in the West Bank; Es-
genoôpteitj, New Brunswick; and in Asubpeeschoseewagong,
Kenora, and Roberstville, Ontario. He lives in Toronto with his
partner, Dan Hunt.

# Sacred Encounters with Wolf

~ *Anita L. Keith* ~

Wolf bays forlornly into the northern sky, framed by the circle of the moon. The winged ones, the crawling ones, the four-legged creatures turn their attention in the direction of the lonely sound. The universe listens as Wolf fills the silence with her mystery song.

Why does Wolf bay at the moon? In aboriginal cultures it is believed that Wolf is the forerunner of new ideas that lie just below the surface of consciousness. Wolf may be telling us to seek out lonely places that will allow us to connect with the Creator. In the aloneness, one may find solace, inspiration, and a connection with the divine.

> If you want to learn, then go and ask
> The wild animals and the birds, the flowers and fish.
> Any of them can tell you what the Lord has done.
> Every living creature is in the hands of God.
> (Job 12:7–10 paraphrased)

A dear friend of mine has a red-haired wolf named Little Girl. This majestic ten-year-old loves to cuddle. She often sits quietly at our feet and enjoys being with us. When I am in her presence, I sense that I am included and safe in the pack. If she is not cuddling with us, she is likely walking the periphery of the yard and house watching over us.

People are usually surprised when I tell them about Little Girl; they don't know that wolves can embrace humans as part of their family. But in the ancient days, it was common for aboriginal people to include wolves as part of their family. Today, they are still revered animals, and it is quite common for us to use ceremonies as a way to learn from wolves and other animals.

I often attend traditional aboriginal women's gatherings. As we find our place within the circle, the drummers begin to play the ancient songs. As the rhythm pulses in our ears, we connect as a group. We connect with Creator. We connect to the ancestors. We connect to the universe. We also connect to animals. We travel into a spiritual dimension where we connect with the wonders of creation. During this meditative state, we allow our minds to ponder the Great Mystery who made all of creation.

I often think about Wolf during these gatherings. I feel an affinity with this animal and have spent hours learning about Wolf so that I might understand her. I have learned how very much like the two-legged ones Wolf can be. For example, I have learned that Wolf is a creature that has a strong urge to be an individual. As humans, we too have the ability to be part of society and yet still embody our individual dreams and ideas.

According to the sacred teachings of our elders, Wolf naturally spends her life travelling to new terrain. When she finds a place she likes, she marks out her territory, her enclosure. There was a time when the land was plentiful; but in the present day, Wolf must fight for space and food. What were once endless tracts of land with their wide boundaries have now been reduced to enclosed spaces where Wolf and her family must dwell.

In our more recent experience of living in nature with Wolf, however, our elders are telling a story of a significant change. The land is no longer plentiful, and Wolf and her family now have to fight for space and food. Many live in the same space, which disrupts their migration and social patterns. An entire generation of Young Wolves was born inside the very limited space available for wildlife. They do not know what it is like to travel freely to find new territories. They are being pressed in on all sides by new freeways, urban sprawl, and new settlements. A longing develops within the Young Wolves. Sensing there is something missing, they seek out the older wolves and ask what it used to be like outside their boundaries. They want to find that which was lost—freedom, adventure, control of their destiny and life.

Some Young Wolves choose to leave and enter the space of humans. In this new territory, they settle and raise their families. In many ways, they are free at last—to roam, to find new terrain, to seek out food. But with this new space comes new dangers. The two-legged ones, upon sight of the Young Wolves, instinctively hunt them down in order to protect their families, their farm animals, their hiking trails. Hunted day and night, the Young Wolves fear they will not live much longer.

Unfortunately, once they break with the original pack, the Young Wolves cannot go back. The alpha wolves, the dominant male and female of the pack, have resettled the land and the territory now belongs to them. Because a wolf pack has a definite social structure and rules of conduct, re-entry would mean another confrontation with life and death. For the Young Wolves, danger lurks everywhere.

The story of Wolf is a teaching tool for the elder. At the end of the story, the elder may ask, "How then does Young Wolf fulfill her calling?" If taught in a women's circle, this is where the story becomes surprisingly powerful. As one actively seeks to meditate and learn from Wolf, one begins to realize that Wolf's wisdom and intuition empowers the teacher within us to come forth and help us, the two-legged ones, in understanding the Great Mystery.

As I think of the plight of Wolf within the limited space in which she must now survive, I can identify with her. To learn from Wolf, we must allow Wolf's wisdom to be personal, affecting our identity, sense of belonging, and hidden fears. We enter into her story, a story that parallels our own life experiences.

As I reflect on Our Maker Loving and the Holy Scripture, great people of the Bible come to mind. I think of Abraham and Sarah in the book of Genesis and wonder what they would have done if they were challenged with the plight of Wolf. Abraham and Sarah belonged to a country, a culture, a family. They knew who they were. They understood what was expected of them. The command to go forth to a new land presented them with a difficult choice. Should they remain in the place of their ancestors with their identity intact and their place in society secured, or should they listen to God and set out, not knowing where they were going?

One never has to face exclusion when one is secure within one's family and community. The new generation of Young Wolves who had lived inside the enclosed space for so long had a sense of belonging as well, but something was missing. A yearning burned within them. They too were called to greatness, to fulfill their life's journey. After a time, however, their sense of belonging turned to exclusion. Inside the enclosure, they were barred from exploring and living in the larger world that existed outside their enclosed terrain. Outside the enclosure, too, they were excluded—they could not return.

The plight of Young Wolves reminds us how subtly we too can be drawn into situations where we feel safe and cared for while in reality, we may be held back from exploring new horizons. In life, there are many invisible structures that we live within. They might be the expectations that our families place on us or the unwritten rules in an organization. They might be peer pressure or the sense of rejection that arises because we are overweight or not a part of a cool group. Especially for those of us who know ourselves as children of the living God, we understand fully that earth is not our home. Like Abraham and Sarah, we are sojourners.

Abraham and Sarah had their spiritual beliefs and heritage, but in many ways God was calling them to move away from their community and into a new destiny with God. Abraham and Sarah chose to leave. In cutting the ties that so profoundly defined them and departing from the land of their ancestors, they would forge a path for the heirs that were to come, blessing others. As Christians, we too must find the journey that Creator has designated especially for us, and we must travel it. This is accomplished by having our ear attuned to Our Maker Loving, the One who made us and directs us to Christ.

I also feel a certain kinship with another hero of Scripture, the Apostle Paul. He reminds me of Lone Wolf. Lone Wolf belongs to the pack and has a strong sense of family, as well as a strong urge to be an individual. One may feel a sense of sadness for Lone Wolf people because they are unaccompanied so much of the time. And yet, that is a part of who they are. Setting oneself apart is a must for those of us who seek Christ with a deep hunger. I can imagine Paul, much like Lone Wolf, stealing away to find time with God, to seek the presence of the Holy Spirit. As Lone Wolf communes mysteriously with nature, so too we must find those times of solitude to renew and refresh ourselves in God.

Paul would have left with the Young Wolves, but he longed for freedom for others as well. Today, as during the days of the early church, many people sit on the fence—somewhere between returning to their former, sinful way of life and moving forward in the freedom in Christ. These are the weak ones in the Body of Christ. In some ways they are like the sick and elderly within the pack—too weak to help themselves. Wolf, true to her nature, stays close by and looks after them. She returns time and again with food. She watches over them to protect them. Abraham and Sarah and Paul transcended their place and identity within their cultures and communities. They moved past their positions and placement in the world and took up their cross, leaving the safety of their own personal enclosure.

Another thing that Wolf teaches is how to face death. Aboriginal people believe that it is important to die well. This self-control in the face of death earns a warrior the greatest *orenda*—personal power. This way of thinking is similar to the mentality of Wolf when she hunts. Wolf has an unspoken conversation with her prey about death. When predator and prey first meet, the outcome of the hunt is usually settled in the first moment, the moment of eye contact between the two. What transpires between those moments of staring between predator and prey is probably a complex exchange of information regarding the

appropriateness of the chase and the kill. This encounter is the
conversation of death.

This reminds me of the chance meeting I had with Wolf as a
child. I was nine years old and was walking near my home on the
outskirts of town. As I neared the top of the hill, I saw something
standing in the distant field. It was Wolf. For a moment our eyes
locked. I looked toward home, which was about fifty yards away,
and I looked back at Wolf. I knew instinctively that if I ran, I
would not make it. There it was—a brush with life and death.
In that split second, I decided to look away and keep walking for
home. Wolf continued on her journey. With Wolf, there needs
to be that ritual and choice. Predator and prey grow stronger
together by means of the single encounter.

Paul had many encounters with death. How many times did
he look his predator in the eye? How many times did he defeat
death? What were the thoughts going through his mind each
time? Did he walk away stronger? Did it build his resolve and
commitment to Christ? Encounters with death are good teachers. There are lessons that we learn dramatically in those few
seconds. The fleeting nature of our life is glaringly apparent and
we again come to the cold awareness that death's icy grip would
take us out in a moment if it were not for Christ, our mainstay
and shelter in the storm.

Unfortunately for Wolf and the Young Wolves, their dwelling
space has grown smaller. There are no more horizons to seek out,
and food is scarce. Some have left the small spaces. The elderly
and sickly remain inside. Others live on the periphery. It is time
to rethink where we are at. In our personal enclosures, are we
feeling settled or constrained? Are we like the elderly in need of
shelter and care? Are we like the Young Wolves, tempted to fear-
lessly head off into the hills with no regard for others and to seek
out new adventures? Do we stay inside because it is familiar? Do
we vacillate on the periphery? Do we know when our personal
enclosures have become unhealthy with impossible expectations

placed on us? As Christians, what high calling are we being drawn toward?

When we look at Wolf, we see many parallels with our own lives. The lessons we learn from Wolf will be different for each one of us. Her teaching brings us to a crossroads in our personal journey. What can Wolf teach us now?

---

Anita L. Keith, a member of the Algonquin/Mohawk aboriginal community, is an instructor in Aboriginal Education at Red River Community College in Winnipeg, where she lives. She is author of *For Our Children Our Sacred Beings, Sacred Children Sacred Teachers*, and *Sacred Learning*. An ordained minister, she is a consultant with the North American Institute of Indigenous Theological Studies and with My People International. Anita travels internationally, speaking to organizations and churches on aboriginal issues. She has three adult children and four grandchildren.

# Growing Up Here, and There
~ *Mark Buchanan* ~

I grew up here, though "here" traverses a scattered terrain: Calgary's balmy chinooks and icy winds, the Cariboo's snow and mosquitoes, Vancouver's rain and glitter, north Okanagan's snaky deserts, south Okanagan's fragrant orchards, Vancouver Island's ferny wilderness. Maybe it's better to say I grew up here, and there. It's as though I've lived in half a dozen countries in one lifetime. My father worked for an oil company and every few years, at the stroke of some faceless executive's pen, we were emigrants again. Our lives were semi-nomadic, never settled, never rooted. That bred in my bones wanderlust, steeped in my blood restlessness. I am a stranger in a strange land.

Biblical characters—the patriarchs, Moses, Nehemiah, Paul, and more—moved a lot too. Their stories are blurs of motion. For all their closeness to the land—land was identity, promise, safeguard, inheritance, legacy, heirloom, buffer—few of them stayed in one place long. War or restlessness, skulduggery or fam-ine, forced exile or chosen banishment, or simply and deeply the sheer irresistible call of Yahweh, meant that they were sojourners more than settlers. If Adam the farmer, born to tend one place, is in our blood, so is his son Cain, the restless wanderer, cursed to be nowhere at home. Even Joshua, namesake of Jesus, called to settle Canaan, was told by God, "I will be with you wherever you go."

A wayfarer's creed, that.

Which seems the creed of Jesus, too. He had no fixed ad-dress, was a vagabond and refugee. His parents were forced by faceless executives to stay on the move. In adulthood, he went from village to village, town to town, never knowing in the morning where he'd lay his head that night. He promises to settle us in the promised land, to build mansions for us there so we can finally burn our tents, but was himself a restless wanderer, cruci-fied, as Hebrews say, "outside the camp." His blood is better than Abel's, but he also bore the curse of Cain.

I am almost fifty and I've lived now for more than a dozen years and in one house on south Vancouver Island. This is the longest I've stayed one place. I love it here and hope, especially on my good days, that God in his mercy lets me remain. I can picture my gravestone here.

Why not? I can drive five minutes and be in a seaside fishing village, eating fresh whole-grain bread baked two doors down, feasting on scaly or spiny things fetched from the bay I gaze out on, drinking hypnotically rich coffee roasted on the island I look across at. The water in my glass comes from one of our many mountain lakes, and is pristine as first love. The wine on the table is made from grapes grown not more than a good walk's distance from here, and is world-class. Or I can drive ten minutes in the other direction and be in rain-drenched forest, alone except for deer, bears, skunks, raccoons, cougars, and eagles, in silence except for the wind in the high boughs and the rivers sweeping across stones. Or I can leave in the morning and by noon be on the west coast, watching waves fantail off rocks, prying moon shells from the sand, making a fire on the beach from driftwood. This is as close to Eden as this broken world gets.

But I'm never quite at home. In this replica of paradise I still dream of elsewhere and otherwise. Any given day, without rhyme or rhythm, I might chafe at the weather, carp at my work, long to be elsewhere. I imagine that if I could be some other place, doing some other thing, I'd finally be happy.

This might very well be a character flaw, aggravated by my upbringing. But I wonder. I wonder if what it really is, or mostly is, is the paradox of the Christian faith.

The Christian faith is both settling and unsettling, a homecoming and an exile. It is a call to life's abundance, an invitation to savour earth's many gifts—marriage and children, friends and books, coffee and calypso, dancing and sleeping, and sex and pizza. But it's a call away from all that, too. Following Jesus grounds me in this life and yet weans me from it. He invites me to rest and exhorts me to keep moving.

Jesus tells those of us who follow him that we'll find three things: life to the full, rest for our soul, and a cross on our back. We'll find our life by losing it. We'll inherit the earth only to discover that this world is not our home. We'll fix our eyes upon Jesus, and run with perseverance. We'll turn our eyes upon Jesus, and the things of this earth will grow strangely dim.

We'll live well in the land.

But always, and more and more, we'll wish we were elsewhere.

$\sim$

My wife and I celebrated our twenty-second anniversary recently. Twenty-two years of marriage is no great landmark, but it feels like a feat. We're still more or less the same size and shape we were when we married, but softer, stiffer, more pleated versions of that. My hair has moulted from my head and sprouted out my ears. Our skin parches and loosens. Our children, just brought home, it seems, from the maternity ward, now drive cars, roll their eyes at our slowness and gibberish, and wish they were with friends.

So twenty-two years, though no milestone, deserved some marking out, some small act of self-congratulation. We rented a log cabin on the west coast for three nights, and one Sunday afternoon we left from church and drove a road that twists and climbs and dips and sets you down, dizzy and queasy, on one of the most spectacular stretches of waterfront in the world. The cabin was just above a protected cove. At low tide, that cove became an archipelago of rocks encrusted with barnacles and starfish, tidal pools filled with anemones and crabs. Evening was coming on, and it was cool and cloudy, so we made a fire in the stone hearth. When night came, we slipped into the hot tub. The

wind had pulled the clouds off the stars, stark and mysterious
as revelations, and we gazed upward, silent with joy. The next
morning we slept late, then ventured from beach to beach, falling asleep once, like lost orphans, amidst the piles of driftwood
that edge the coastline. In the evening, we cooked steaks and
potatoes on the barbecue.

I could happily have lived there for ever. Yet when the day
came to leave, I was just as happy to go.

Following Jesus means that you're happy to stay and happy
to leave. Any place can become home, and none. Jesus helps us
love the earth more and the world less. He deepens our capacity
to cherish and relish simple things and yet slowly weans us from
our cravings, our dependencies, our expectations. He mends us
in places we didn't know we were broken and breaks us in places
where, before his advent, we were utterly content. We start
to enjoy more and demand less. Almost everything feels like a
gift, not a possession, not an entitlement. He teaches us to live
with our hands open, wide open, and our arms, too, so that we
receive more but lose more as well.

As well.

☙

Last year, Carol died. Carol was my colleague for ten years and
my wife's closest friend. She had a wanderlust too. She'd lived in
many places and travelled to more, and restlessness was always
a dull rumble beneath her contentment. We knew that we were
going to lose her even before she was diagnosed with the cancer
that, after a long valiant battle, took her life: she had fallen in
love with Rwanda. Her heart was with its joyful, sorrowing
people. That place had claimed her as its own.

Then she got sick and didn't get better, though many moments we thought she would. Always, we prayed she would.
She was barely forty and prodigiously gifted, and it made no

clear sense to us why God needed her more than we did. After she died, I wrote a tribute to her in the local paper and ended by saying Carol was finally home. A Christian woman sent me a response. She told me I should be ashamed of myself and embarrassed to call myself a pastor. The reason Carol died, she said, was that we—I, my wife, our church—lacked sufficient faith. Carol's death was on our hands, because, this woman said, the God *she* worshipped *always* heals.

I didn't respond because I couldn't think of a kind way to do so. I was angry. Mostly, I was puzzled. I couldn't make heads or tails out of her claim that God *always* heals. The statistics on death, George Bernard Shaw said, are impressive. And I'm unaware of any time in history when death's seeming randomness—striking saints in their prime and missing tyrants in theirs, snatching the young in their nimbleness while the old languish in decrepitude—was, well, less random.

I've yet to notice that following Jesus is a surefire way to avoid life's heartache.

But it does mean that you're happy to stay and happy to leave. Carol was, for most of her illness, happy to stay. By the end, she was happy to leave. But I think that all her illness did was bring into sharp relief what was deep in her heart anyway, what is deep in the heart of all who love the man of sorrows and the prince of peace: we love it here, but long for elsewhere. Carol's epitaph is Philippians 1:21—"To live is Christ; to die is gain."

A wayfarer's creed, that.

❧

My friend and fellow writer Marshall Shelley has had two children die. One was mere minutes into daylight, and then slipped into darkness. The other was two years old.

It's hard. There is no simple way to explain that. There are no easy comforts. Long after it happened, but not that long, he wrote about it, and dared to ask why God would make anyone to live for just two years, or just two minutes? His answer is stunning in its simplicity and profoundness. God made *no one* to live for two minutes, or two years, or twenty, or forty, or eighty-six.

He made people to live forever.

To love it here, but long for elsewhere. To grow up here, and there.

---

Mark Buchanan is a pastor and the author of five books, most recently *The Rest of God* and *Hidden in Plain Sight*.
He lives with his wife, Cheryl, and their three children on Vancouver Island, British Columbia.

# The Cross and the Sword Trial—
# Confronting the Mystery of Love of
# Enemy
*~ Leonard Desroches ~*

*Leonard Desroches and two other men were tried in April 2000 for their attempt, the previous Good Friday, to remove a sword affixed to a stone cross at Toronto's St. Paul's Anglican Church. They had been charged with the criminal offence of "Mischief over $5,000." The three, who included Catholic priest Bob Holmes, and Dan Heap, Anglican priest and former Member of Parliament, were supported in court by one hundred priests, nuns, war veterans, activists, teachers, and students. Visibly affected, the judge granted each an "absolute discharge."*

Over the years, at least three different neighbours have seriously threatened me. One threatened my life for confronting serious abuse on our street. I've been disowned for refusing to disown a neighbour's enemy. Some have purposely broken my things. One slashed the tires of my bike and extinguished a lit cigarette on its seat. A number have lied to me. Some have stolen from me. Some have pounded on walls and ceilings in an attempt to intimidate a fellow neighbour. One young neighbour on heavy drugs threw garbage on my doorstep and yelled, "I'll get you," because I had finally removed his motorcycle parts from my entrance (as he had promised to do over and over). These are all "ordinary Canadians."

In each case I have challenged myself to do all I could to live the mystery of love of enemy. Because of that, I have grown spiritually. Many times my neighbour-enemy has been my teacher, revealing my own anger and fear. In all cases, I have renounced the quest for victory and have worked for reconciliation, for some transformation of the conflict at hand. Because of that, I have become freer. In each case, there has indeed been a transformation of the conflict—sometimes to a dramatic degree. The young man who dumped garbage at my entrance and harassed me for days came up to me unexpectedly and apologized—actually admitting, "I have been on drugs for the last while," and showing me some child-like drawings he had just done.

Freedom has always been one of the greatest mysteries to me. We are free to love and we are free to hate. However difficult the choice may be, it remains a choice. The mystery of freedom encounters what at first seems merely a moral imperative: love your enemy. And yet, more fully understood, it is the mystery of freedom encountering the mystery of love of enemy. Mystery encountering mystery.

Mysteries are to be lived. We are not *as* One Body, we *are* One Body. When one part is hurt, all are hurt. We are that intimately connected—lover, friend, or enemy. Yet we are free; free to destroy or to nurture interdependence. The most sanctioned rupture is the one between myself and my enemy. The most illusionary freedom is that which is based on the destruction of the enemy. The most radical freedom is the freedom found at the very heart of the mystery of love of enemy. And the enemy is everywhere— stranger, neighbour, co-worker, parent, spouse, child, lover, or self. To be fully alive is to live the mystery of freedom at the very heart of the mystery of love of enemy; to do the emotional and spiritual work involved—individually and collectively; to enter more deeply into the depth and breadth of Love.

Slowly, I am unlearning the lie of my culture: love of enemy is not sexy; it does not sell; it is for naive weaklings. Slowly, I am unlearning the lie of the official church: love of enemy is just an ideal, an optional challenge to reach for the impossible in one's private life. At most, love of enemy is presented as a command only, not as a life-giving mystery. Slowly, I am learning that not to live the mystery of love of enemy is to be seriously stunted in spirit, in vision, and in imagination. This mystery affects all we do—including our work of hospitality and resistance. To offer hospitality and to do resistance—even radical hospitality and radical resistance—from the wrong motives is spiritually unhealthy and dangerous. When hospitality or resistance is disconnected from love of enemy, what is it really about? When the crises and conflicts surface, will we have the spiritual resources needed?

"But you're just a drywaller! What do you know about mysteries?" If these mysteries are not accessible to all of us, we are doomed.

"But you're a nice Canadian, not an 'ugly American.' Isn't your resistance extreme?" Our lying myth of "Canada the peacemaker" keeps us in dangerous denial about the particular nature of Canadian militarism: cowardly acquiescence to the empire and hypocritical profiteering. War simply cannot be left to the self-proclaimed experts—military and political.

Every culture has a warrior tradition: Christian, Jewish, Muslim, and Buddhist; Francophone Canadian, Anglophone Canadian, and First Nations; Conservative Party, Liberal Party, and New Democratic Party. Historically we are all confronted with the same challenge: to perpetuate the institution of war or to begin a global apprenticeship in the other force. In a culture where the many do not confront the enemy within, the few are eventually sent to destroy the designated enemy without.

The more I pray for a deepening compassion, the less willing I become to expend my energy reacting to the endless wars; the more I need to resist War itself. The more I try to stretch in faith, the more central a mystery love of enemy reveals itself to be.

A good Jesuit friend who had seriously considered joining our Cross and Sword witness at St. Paul's Anglican Church expressed his hesitation by referring to the war memorial with the cross and sword as a "dead symbol." Others referred to it as "*just* a symbol."

A symbol is fully a symbol—not "just" a symbol. It may represent something significant or something quite insignificant. For me, the Cross and Sword symbol was as significant as a statue depicting Christ napalming a child, raping an enemy, tortur-

ing a prisoner of war, or starving the already poor by throwing
the people's money (taxes) down a sewer. The symbol of the
Cross and Sword war memorial is that real for me. It is not just
a symbol; it is *fully* a symbol of the blasphemy of war and of who
we have become as mainline churches. It remains intact, well
protected by state and church.

Confronting the Cross and Sword symbol was for me
emotionally akin to the unearthing of mass graves. Both around
the war memorial and over the mass graves, grass and flowers
hide corruption. Not long ago, a colour photo in the *Toronto Star*
depicted a man and a woman trying to identify relatives amongst
bound and mutilated corpses from a mass grave in Chechnya.
The woman covers her mouth and nose with a cloth. The man
has a full gas mask on. The terrible corruption beneath the quiet
facade of grass and flowers has been exposed. Is the Cross and
Sword a "dead symbol," or have we, as a culture, become spiritually numb?

Sometimes the wheels inside my brain and heart grind like
bits of glass and blood at the sight of the relentless war-making.
After centuries of cheap prayers and expensive taxes, we have
nearly perfected our killing machine: women and minorities are
allowed into its ranks and offered a free career; a bottomless pit
of taxpayers' money assures the ceaseless perfection of war's
technology; and a perpetual war economy is so normalized that
even the most progressive economists rarely make the connections between militarism and the globalization of poverty. Most
mainstream economists build their impressive-sounding logic on
sick premises, such as the expendability of the poor.

I never, ever, chose this vocation of exposing and resisting War. It—Christ—kept confronting me. Resisting war has
disrupted my life and those around me as surely as joining the
war-making would have. The hardest thing is that my personal-
ity does not lean toward "being against" or "resisting," but rather
toward creating. I would rather spend my time doing works of

mercy—without having to cry out; doing good work—without having to expose militarism; creating beauty—without facing my culture's sickness.

Recently, I was relishing the energy of live music. Its raw power suddenly sliced through me, like a sharp knife, exposing vulnerable emotions: "What have I been doing all these years resisting War—instead of creating music, growing gardens?" So many "failures." So few "successes." So little personal "security."

And yet, I experience an indestructible joy, beyond any temporary happiness. I experience fruitfulness, beyond all successes or failures. The war child left at the doorway of my soul long ago has taken me into the life-giving mystery of love of enemy. She has the most urgent message of all to give to my culture about poverty and freedom. I have learned that the same One who is with the War Child in her unjust suffering and death will be with me in my own suffering and death. Put simply, freedom has taken root in me.

I have learned that no prison can take that freedom away. Nor can the threat of death. I can think of no greater honour than to die resisting war. Yet it is not at all what I most desire. What *do* I desire? My desire is freedom—far beyond the bloodied walls of fear and hatred of enemy erected by prison or church; far beyond myself and my small community of friends. My desire is for the freedom of the whole of the Beloved Community. Directly connected to this desire for freedom is my love for the church community.

My love for the church is—like my love of God—either an irrelevant sentiment or a vital part of being fully human: living a relationship with God in community with sisters and brothers for the love of all humanity and all creation. I dearly love my widest community: friends who know nothing of the church's inner riches; friends who can only feel the hurt that the church represents; friends of other faiths. But I have a burning love for the sheer mystery of church as faith community. My soul needs the nourishment found in this mystical, indestructible home. It is where I live my greatest freedom.

Leonard Desroches has published many articles and three books on the spirituality and practice of non-violence: *Allow the Water*; *Love of Enemy: The Cross and Sword Trial*; and *Spiritualité et pratique de la non-violence*. Len has been a trainer for Christian Peacemaker Teams and Peace Brigades International, and was a founder of the former independent newspaper *Catholic New Times*. A drywall taper by trade, he lives with his spouse, Anna, and son, Luc, in Toronto.

# Facing Outward, Looking Up
~ *Lorna Dueck* ~

When I arrived in Toronto's television market, a burly, self-important man with title and prestige impolitely told me I looked like a deer caught in the headlights. He laughed out loud at me, and made me feel small and stupid. I really was not a television viewer and the medium mattered little to me; did anyone care what was on the screen?

Yet I was on coveted and sacred ground in this TV world, and Toronto was about to educate me. Everything about the city intimidated me and made me feel a stranger, with loneliness my only companion. Until one day early after my move, when I noticed Toronto's population sign: 2.3 million twigged a familiar story. Moses had led just over two million people from Egypt into God's promised land. Somehow I seemed to feel the Spirit of God soothe my soul, assuring me that in the noisy and rude mass of people among whom I had landed, individuals did matter.

What a mystery it has been to be invited into the multi-ethnic mix to look for evidence of God's love, using a medium greatly unsuited in its demand for brevity and entertainment to the depth and wonder of Jesus. There have been endless lessons to learn from others on the journey—like the email that requested my help in making vegetarian chili to feed 300 Buddhist monks for a picnic at Toronto's lakeside. A media-frenzied visit from the Dalai Lama was causing this call to hospitality. As a reporter, I could see that the Dalai Lama held up a mirror to us, and in the reflection was a country that still loves the energy of discovering ways to "nurture a good heart." In post-Christian Canada I found myself jealously admiring a vibrant, wrinkled monk who often seemed to giggle. My worry was that my own activism in the Christian world would cause me to stop laughing.

I'm caught in a world famous for overburdened, unavailable clergy rather than one famous for the words of Jesus: "Don't worry about tomorrow." These words aren't celebrated much in the technology-laden paths that mark my way. "Come to me all you who are weary and burdened and I will give you rest" are the words of my master, Jesus, so why is my life always gasping for air?

What a wonderful Saviour that he should give us a Lord's Prayer focused on making room for the vastness of God amid activities of earthbound life and our material needs. It seems the pursuit of Christianity has been perceived to be too small for the largeness of life that Canadians need to live. I couldn't disagree more with that perception, and so I argue it out in public.

It's in that tension that I find myself on our show *Listen Up*, week after week, delighted to find evidence that this journey with God is still a conversation for the public places of TV, newspaper, and the web. In covering the best of stories, I find myself caught again like a deer in the headlights in utter astonishment, discovering new manifestations of God with us.

Like the time I stood on charred earth in Barriere, British Columbia, where a forest fire had wiped out an area twice the size of Toronto. I interviewed Mike Barre, who had been convicted of starting the fire when he carelessly dropped his cigarette. With neighbours made homeless, and with lumber-related employment wiped out for most of the community, Mike was almost going mad with guilt, when God interrupted him. Introduced to an eternally optimistic Pentecostal preacher and Mennonite volunteers rebuilding the area, Mike discovered the power of story circles within which to process the mystery of God in us. A few months later, Mike stood in the icy waters of a lake surrounded by charred forest and was baptized into Christian commitment.

God with us. I like it best when I find the wonder of that truth in the news that shapes our world.

I saw it again in John and Liane Niles, a Markham, Ontario, couple that has taken in more than a thousand foster kids in the last twenty years. Their home is a front-line destination for Toronto police as they apprehend children from scenes of abuse and crime. John, a United Church minister, says the city's children are coming to them in increasingly worse shape—brutalized, broken, and evidencing the worst of what evil can do to them.

When I met Rev. Niles, he was president of Toronto's prestigious Empire Club, where the who's who of the country's business and political elite vie for a speaker's podium with lunchtime crowds. Few knew of his passion to challenge Canadians to create soft landing places for children in crisis. His own five children created the concept of Kits for Kids, launching a process that makes thousands of knapsacks loaded with age-appropriate gifts for displaced Canadian kids.

My favourite story of the Niles' incarnational living happened one Christmas. Rev. Niles recalls how a young ward we'll call Nelson took a liking to the family's nativity set. Nelson kept playing with it, putting the baby Jesus in his pocket, walking about, then carefully putting it back. When Nelson left their home, the family could no longer find the baby in the manger. "Daddy, I think Nelson took Jesus with him," said one of the Niles children. "I do hope he did," said the Reverend.

That is the other side of the frantic, outward Christianity we have been called to. We have a gift that the world can take with it. Delighted, yet at times terrified to talk about this in the media, I still find it a wonder to be called to interpret faith in public spaces.

Amid the noise, the experience is grounded in the journey inward. I'm laughably old-fashioned, as most mornings will find me in an upholstered rocking chair with an afghan, my Bible, and journal, and often a newspaper. It's a long and unhurried journey, taking time for prayers that are deep, nourishing, and wonderfully quiet in their silence.

Lorna Dueck began her career in Christian broadcasting in 1994 and in 2004 founded a weekly news and current events television program called *Listen Up TV*. Its title was meant to say, "Listen to the world and look up." It is seen Sunday mornings on Global TV across Canada, and on numerous specialty channels. Lorna lives in Burlington, Ontario. She and her husband, Vern, have two grown children out exploring the world.

Transformation

# Accidents of Birth
~ *John Fraser* ~

The day Pauline Vanier died in Compiègne earlier this year
at the great age of ninety-one, Shen Zhong-hua slammed his
dilapidated bicycle into a delivery van at the foot of a hill on
Christie Street in Toronto. The two events are hitched in my
mind because, seconds after I had hung up on the long-
distance call from Madame Vanier's son Jean, in France, my
sister called to say Mr. Shen was in hospital getting a broken leg
put in a cast. He had been charged with reckless driving, she
added, and the van owner was demanding exorbitant damages.

Grieve for the dead, worry about the living: life sometimes
comes in bizarre clumps. Mammy, as Pauline Vanier was called
by everyone who was close to her in her last two or three decades, lived a life as full as anyone's in the old Canada. Consort
to the only truly great governor general Canada has ever had,
Georges-Philéas Vanier, she had "retired" to a small village outside Compiègne to live out her last years at the mother house of
the international L'Arche movement for mentally handicapped
adults founded by Jean Vanier. The terminal illness lasted less
than a week and then her mighty spirit fled her body.

Mr. Shen is only thirty-eight and was born into a poor
Chinese peasant family in Shanxi province, the fourth of six
children and the only one in the entire history of his family to
get a higher education. An agronomist, he was on an exchange
visit to Canada at the time of the Tienanmen slaughter and
virtually jumped into our arms when my sister made the mis-
take of expressing some concern over his plight. Since I once
worked as a journalist in China, I bear the heavy burden of being the Chinese expert in the family, and before long Mr. Shen
and either my sister or I were to be seen making the dogged
rounds of immigration and manpower offices in Toronto.

Mammy died surrounded by people who loved her for
herself and for all that her remarkable life represented. Her

sons and daughter were nearby. A network of people associated with the L'Arche movement around the world held vigils
in her honour and cradled her in their hearts on her final passage. In Toronto, Mr. Shen is for practical purposes all alone
save for our family, which is small comfort in the night when
he goes about his work at a twenty-four-hour gas station.

The job comes complete with illegally low wages and a
boss who cheats him of a few dollars most weeks by alleging
accounting inaccuracies. Since Mr. Shen never makes mistakes
with money, this is more than a grievance: it strikes at his
sense of honour and fairness. There's nothing he can do about
it, though, and he always gives in because he knows—as his
boss knows even better—that there are a dozen people ready
to take his job at any given time.

In his spare moments, Mr. Shen holds down another
(part-time) job, gives volunteer tai chi chuan instruction at a
neighbourhood YMCA, and attends an ever-increasing variety
of self-improvement courses. He lives in a closet of a room in
a boarding house a few blocks from where he had his accident,
buys six-month supplies of staple foods at emporiums I never
knew existed, clothes himself at Goodwill, and never fails to
listen to the *World at Six* on CBC Radio after he has awakened
from the four to five hours' sleep he allows himself six days
out of seven. On Sundays, he does his intensive studying and
his laundry. He writes letters to his wife and two children
back in China, sometimes visits us, and—wherever else he
goes—makes a point of avoiding Chinatown (for reasons
that seem obvious to defecting Chinese and overwrought to
middle-class native Canadians).

The bicycle accident was a catastrophe, a far bigger one
than most of us could even begin to comprehend. He was
returning from the gas-station job. The half-hour ride got him
home around 7:30 a.m., and the leisurely free-wheel down
the final hill was one of the few enjoyable moments. Until,

that is, this particular morning when he applied the brakes
and discovered he didn't have brakes any more. He tried to
slow the bike by skidding along the sidewalk curb and dragging a foot, but everything was happening too fast and the
next thing he knew he had crashed into the parked van and
was splayed on the sidewalk in agony, his right leg twisted at a
queer angle.

The owner of the van never once helped him, but instead
shouted obscenities along with what Mr. Shen described as
"unfriendly" observations on the Chinese race. Within minutes, prompted by a telephone call from the van owner, two
squad cars were on the scene. An officer in the first car talked
to the van owner, then demanded some identification of Mr.
Shen, and finally charged him with reckless driving. An officer
in the second car helped him up and drove him to a hospital.
The crumpled bicycle was abandoned and presumably ended
up in the garbage; it was certainly not returned to Mr. Shen.

The nice cop said that the nasty cop's rap could probably
be beaten, but at this point Mr. Shen wasn't taking too much
in. He was wondering how he could hold on to his two jobs,
how he could avoid disappointing the senior citizens at his tai
chi sessions, how he was going to get to his own classes. He
thought of Chairman Mao's favourite fable, of the old man
who moved a mountain, a parable from Cultural Revolution
theology meant to spur the masses to impossible tasks, but
then ruefully remembered that the old man had two working
legs when he moved all the earth and stone.

A week after she died, Mammy's body was flown back to
Canada for a state funeral in Quebec City. It may be a cliché
to say that funerals are for the living, but clichés, too, are for
the living. My wife and I needed an occasion fixed on some
proximity to her to focus the awful sense of loss. Our friendship had been one of the few pure perquisites of a life in

journalism. On the way to a posting in Beijing nearly fifteen years ago, I had badgered my way into her life on the excuse of an interview. She refused me twice but my wife and I just turned up at her door anyway. She let us step over the threshold. Not a year passed, after the China posting, that we didn't spend time with each other, either here or in France. The telephone bills have been ridiculous. She has held each of my daughters in her arms and the force of her crunching bear hugs is implanted deep in whatever understanding I have of what it means to be truly alive. Nothing was going to keep us away from Quebec City, so my sister volunteered to look after the children. And Mr. Shen.

The Queen sent a wreath. The governor general came. Soldiers of her beloved regiment, the Royal Twenty-Second, ushered people to their seats in the cathedral, bore her body through the nave, and carried it to the vault hollowed out of the rock of the Citadel, where she was placed beside General Vanier. At the service, Jean Vanier said that his mother at her end was no different than she had been throughout the lifetime he had known her. She was a little girl, he said, longing to be loved. That was true enough, but I also remembered when she was in St. John's, Newfoundland, in 1966 and let loose a flash of her Franco-Irish ire at a tree-planting ceremony in Bowring Park. It was less than a year before her husband was to die in office, and a civic official, self-important but no doubt well enough intentioned, roughly and noisily barred a stray ragamuffin from getting a closer look at the viceregal couple. Eyes flashing with anger, Mammy left her husband and barged past the official to get to the child. She jackknifed her large frame to bring herself to his level and, in the subsequent brief encounter—a gesture to be sure—she transformed the circle of onlookers into penitents in the cause of simple decency.

After the burial, the regimental band of the Van Doos played "O Canada" and the regiment marched past the crypt.

It seemed that in burying Mammy Vanier we were also sealing up a notion of Canada in the cold stone high above the St. Lawrence River. The notion is hard to express without sounding maudlin, but you could point to the old lady and say, "She was it."

Mr. Shen's court date was twice postponed. He turned up alone both times at the courthouse at the old city hall in Toronto and was sent away both times. The van owner and the police constables—the "witnesses"—never seemed to be there and inquiries by Mr. Shen simply led to a new date. The business left him confused but unbowed. It was while he was preparing for his third date that he finally told my sister what was going on. She phoned me and the two of us immediately called an emergency meeting with him.

We told Mr. Shen that he must have a lawyer. He wouldn't hear of it. He had already somehow insinuated himself into the library of Osgoode Hall Law School and read everything connected to reckless-driving charges. Lawyers, he announced, were too expensive. I had learned by this time not to proffer money, as either gift or loan. He was extremely proud of his independence and the few dollars he had been forced to accept from me when he first made his penniless decision to try to remain in Canada had been returned within three months—with interest (calculated at the prevailing rates, which he had checked out with two banks and a trust company).

He also confided to my sister and me that if he didn't have to go to prison he would be bringing out his wife and children under the Canada-China family reunification program. We tried to disengage him from this wildly premature scheme. While Mr. Shen had shown ingenuity in holding on to both his jobs since the accident, despite crutches and with even less sleep, he was clearly not sufficiently well set up to cope with the considerable extra burden of the family. My sister and I know a lot about these sorts of things.

"I think it's all right," said Mr. Shen quietly. "I've saved fifteen ..."

"For heaven's sake," we said to him, "do you have any idea what it will cost just to fly them here? Fifteen hundred dollars might bring one of them."

"Not fifteen hundred," he said, still quietly. "Fifteen thousand."

"*Fifteen thousand!*" we exclaimed. "That's one, five, and three zeroes."

"Yes," he said, and he smiled this time. "One-five-zero-zero. I've saved it. I think it's enough to get started. My wife's English is not very good, so she will have to go to school for six months before she starts a job."

My sister and I stared at each other, our collective debts crashing against Mr. Shen's fiscal acuity. Together, without saying a word, we retreated from the role of advisers, though we had the grace to keep ourselves—at least for the moment—from soliciting financial advice.

The next day, Mr. Shen and I met outside the courthouse fifteen minutes before he had been told to turn up. He was clutching a file which contained various papers he was going to use in his defence. Everything had been copied by hand from the law books. He had gone over them with us the night before and it was all perfectly incomprehensible. My sister and I had quietly worked it out that, if things went badly, I would try to intervene and get another stay in the proceedings so we could hire a bloody lawyer. That was as close to a strategy as we could come up with.

Together Mr. Shen and I entered the courthouse and found our way, through a jungle of well-dressed lawyers and their nervous clients, to the designated courtroom. It was a woman who was presiding on the bench. We arrived just as she was pronouncing her verdict on some hapless youth and she was severe with him. She seemed in an irritable mood. Truly, the karma was not good. Mr. Shen had begun shaking quite visibly the moment we walked through the portals and, as he sat beside me, we might as well have been hooked up by electrodes, so completely had he transmitted his terror.

Shortly after 3 p.m., a court official called for "Mr."— (long pause) "Shungagungawhee" and told him to approach the bench. The judge looked down at me and asked Mr. Shen if I was his legal counsel. "No," I said, almost in a whisper. I was really upset. "I'm his friend. I guess I'm his sponsor."

She snorted. Or at least it sounded to me like a snort.

Mr. Shen was sworn in. He looked very small before the judge's bench. I had the impression of his slowly being engulfed by the whole setting.

"What's that you're holding?" Her Honour asked peremptorily, pointing to Mr. Shen's file of papers. "Let me see it."

The papers were taken by the court official and handed to the judge. After reading some documentation of her own, she spent an agonizing two minutes perusing Mr. Shen's file before handing it back.

"Well?" she said to the official. The tone was unmistakably brusque.

"Your Honour," he said. "The witnesses are not here."

"Of course they're not," she said. Her eyes were … angry. Very angry. "This man has already had his case postponed twice. What an introduction to our justice system." She rearranged her papers. "You're free to go, sir."

Mr. Shen was locked into his position. His head swivelled toward me, but his feet couldn't turn. The court official approached him. "You can go," he said.

I got up and went to the bar and motioned. "Come on," I hissed, "let's get out of here."

"I'm free?" Mr. Shen asked.

"You're free. It's all over."

I know I said that because when Mr. Shen later regaled my sister with what had happened he said that's what I said. All I can really remember is trying to fight back tears. In the judge's face, I had seen Mammy's eyes.

December 1991

--------

John Fraser is an award-winning Canadian journalist and author of eight books, including the international bestseller *The Chinese: Portrait of a People*. He filled a variety of posts at the *Globe and Mail* between 1972 and 1987, including China correspondent and national editor. From 1987 to 1994, he was editor of *Saturday Night* magazine. Currently, he is Master of Massey College, affiliated with the University of Toronto. He is a committed Anglican and has served as Sunday school teacher and rector's warden at St. Clement's-Eglinton in Toronto.

# The Value of Praying a Doxology
~ *Ron Rolheiser* ~

A friend of mine likes to tease the Jesuits about their motto: *For the greater glory of God*. "God doesn't need you to enhance his glory," he likes to kid them. Partly he's right, but the Jesuits are right too: God doesn't need our praises, but we need to give praise, otherwise our lives degenerate into bitterness and violence. Why?

Spiritual writers have always told us that we are either growing or regressing, never neutral. This means that we are either praising someone or demanding we be praised, offering gratitude or muttering in bitterness, blessing or cursing, turning attention away from ourselves or demanding it be focused on us, expressing admiration or demanding it, praying a doxology or doing violence. We are always doing one or the other and it's only by deflecting attention away from ourselves, which is what we do in essence when we give glory to God, that we save ourselves from egoism, jealousy, bitterness, greed, and violence.

It's no accident that when good art depicts someone being martyred, it always depicts the victim's eyes turned upward, toward heaven, while the eyes of those who are doing the killing or watching it are turned in other directions, never upward. A good artist knows that if we don't have our eyes turned heavenward we are involved somehow in violence.

Michael Ondaatje points this out in *Anil's Ghost*. He submits that unless we celebrate a faith or create something in art, we will do violence to somebody: be an artificer or a demon. Praise or create something beyond yourself or fall into the trap of believing that it's your own person that makes the world go round.

Ondaatje's right. Moreover, this isn't an abstract thing. The lesson's simple: unless we're consistently praising somebody or something beyond ourselves we will be consistently speaking words of jealousy, bitterness, and anger. That's in fact our daily experience: we sit around talking with each other and, invariably, unless we're praising someone we're "killing" someone. Gossip, slander, harsh judgment, and vicious comment are often both the tone and substance of our conversations and they're the very antithesis of a doxology, of offering praise to God. Nothing sounds less like a doxology ("Glory be to the Father and to the Son and to the Holy Spirit") than many of our everyday conversations.

The main reason our faith asks us to constantly render glory to God is that the more we praise the less we slander, gossip, or pass judgment. Offering praise to God, and others, is what saves us from bitterness and violence.

And, in the end, overcoming bitterness and violence is the greatest spiritual hurdle of all. Much tougher than the sixth commandment is the fifth ("Thou Shalt Not Kill!"). As Henri Nouwen used to say, we're killing each other all the time. Nobody is shot by a gun who isn't first shot by a word, and nobody is shot by a word who isn't first shot by a thought. Our thoughts are too frequently murderous and soon enough get expressed in our words: "Who does he think he is!" "She thinks she's so special!" "What a hypocrite!" "She hasn't had an original thought in years!" "It's all about him, isn't it!"

Underneath those comments, driving that bitterness, is a not-so-subtle anxiety and hurt: "What about me? Who's noticing me? Who's giving anything to me?" I say this sympathetically because it's not easy to not be anxious in this way, especially for the young, and it's not easy, after the neuroses of mid-life and beyond, to not be bitter or not feel cheated. For both the young and the old, it's hard to simply say to someone else, God included, "Glory be to you" and really mean it.

We're made in God's image, have a divine fire in us that over-charges us for this world, and live lives of quiet desperation. That desperation, all too often, expresses itself in negative, bitter, and even murderous judgments because the divine in us has been ignored and we feel rage about this slight. But that's precisely why daily, hourly, we need to give glory to God, to pray a doxology. Only by focusing ourselves on the real centre of the universe can we displace ourselves from that centre.

When St. Paul begins his Epistles, he usually does so in a rapture of praise: "Blessed be the God and Father of our Lord Jesus Christ from whose great mercy we all drink!" That isn't a throwaway opening, it's a key part of the main lesson: only by praising something beyond ourselves do we save ourselves from bitterness. All the great spiritual writers do the same. They won't write for long, no matter how bitter or difficult the topic, before they insert some kind of doxology: "Glory be to the Father, the Son, and Holy Spirit." They know a deep secret: only praise saves us from bitterness and only by blessing others do we save ourselves from cursing them.

---

Ron Rolheiser is a Roman Catholic priest and member of the Missionary Oblates of Mary Immaculate. He grew up in Saskatchewan and taught theology and philosophy at Newman Theological College in Edmonton, Alberta. He is the author of eight books, including *Forgotten among the Lilies*, and most recently *Secularity and the Gospel: Being Missionary to Our Children,* and his weekly column is carried in more than sixty-five Catholic papers worldwide. He currently serves as president of Oblate School of Theology in San Antonio, Texas. His website is www.ronrolheiser.com.

# The Child in the Midst

~ *Preston Manning* ~

For three years the Teacher sought to inculcate trust, humility, and the spirit of self-sacrifice among his followers. It was slow going. Now he was taking them to the City where he hoped to impress the importance of these values upon them in a new and unforgettable way.

But as they trudged along the road, his followers began to quarrel vigorously among themselves. It started with an argument over which one of their company would ultimately be "the greatest" of the Teacher's followers. Then it degenerated into heated statements about how "greatness" was to be achieved.

"You must promote yourself," said one, "nobody else will."

"To get ahead, trust no one but yourself," proclaimed another.

"To succeed, always put your own interests ahead of everyone else's," declared a third.

The debate grew louder and more vociferous. A small crowd gathered, including several women with young children. The Teacher spoke quietly to one of the mothers and beckoned the child at her side to come to him. The child came, shy but trusting. The Teacher lifted her gently in his arms, then stepped into the midst of his quarrelling followers.

For a moment they could not disguise their annoyance. They were giving voice to burning ambitions; they were debating important issues of religion and politics. What was the Teacher doing bringing a child into such a situation?

With eyes flashing, the Teacher soon made it plain why he had done so. "This child is trusting," he said. "You should learn to trust like her."

"This child is young and in no position to promote herself or make claims on anyone," he continued. "You should learn the humility of someone in her position.

"You think this little one has no place here and it annoys you that I have made her a place," he concluded. "But I tell you that unless you put the interests of this little one—and others as vulnerable as she—ahead of your own, you have no place in the work I am preparing you for."

As the little band continued on its way, they talked about what had happened. To them it was the presence of the child that had seemed inappropriate, misdirected, and incongruous. But their Teacher had used the child's presence to demonstrate that it was their quarrel that was inappropriate, their ambitions that were misdirected, and their conduct that was incongruous with his intentions for them. Slowly, grudgingly, they began to absorb the lesson of "the child in the midst."

Many years later one of them—a former tax collector named Matthew—wrote the story down. Another member of the group, a fisherman named Peter, retold it to a young man named Mark, who also wrote an account of it, as did a physician named Luke.

The story of "the child in the midst" passed into history. But its capacity to challenge the roots of contemporary quarrels and to refocus contemporary priorities is still potent, if we choose to apply it. Imagine the House of Commons during the daily Question Period—a cauldron of mistrust, ambition, and self-aggrandizement if ever there was one. The Members of Parliament, egged on by the media, are hurling loaded questions, clever retorts, and assorted insults across the floor as usual.

But what if the space between the government and opposition benches were occupied, not by the mace and the tables of the house officers, but by dozens of young children representing more truly than any Member of Parliament the future hopes of our country? Would we politicians be able to act as we so often do, in the face of "the child in the midst"? Would it be the presence and actions of the children that would appear incongruous and out of place in the Commons, or would it be the words and actions of the Members that would now appear inappropriate and misguided?

On a larger and more deadly stage, imagine the road from Ramallah to Jerusalem—a road well travelled by Palestinian militants, Israeli soldiers, and thousands of ordinary people whose lives are being torn asunder by the turmoil and violence of Middle East politics. But what if for one day that road were to be occupied exclusively—from one end to the other—by thousands of children? Palestinian children, Israeli children, children from every nation with a stake in the Middle East conflict?

The suicide bomber who attacked that road would bring down universal censure on his head and his cause. The soldier who fired even one shot in the direction of that road would do the same. For at least a day, that road would know the peace for which most Palestinians and Israelis desperately long.

Closer to home, imagine a contemporary Canadian couple in their twenties or thirties with a precious five-year-old daughter. Somewhere in Mom's and Dad's backgrounds—one generation back, perhaps two or three—there has been a spiritual tradition, maybe Quebec Catholicism, perhaps traditional Judaism, maybe some form of Protestantism, or another faith tradition. But it has been largely lost, swamped by modernity, or maybe jettisoned for good reasons.

One day their little one comes home from kindergarten with a simple but profound question: "Who is Jesus?"

Mom and Dad love the child and are wise enough to realize this is a question that cannot be casually dismissed. The simple question starts them on a journey of reflection and spiritual discovery, addressing the all-important questions: What do they themselves believe? And what beliefs do they intend to pass on to their children? They are challenged as never before by the child in their midst.

The same men who recorded the original story of the child in the midst recorded another story—about angels appearing to shepherds and saying: "There is born to you this day in the city of David a Saviour who is Christ the Lord. And this will be the sign to you: you will find the babe wrapped in swaddling clothes lying in a manger."

Members of the political and religious establishment of that day reacted to the presence of that child by hardening their hearts  and turning away from what he represented. But the shepherds, the wise men, and many of the common people responded by receiving him into their lives.

We remember and repeat this story at Christmas time. It is the challenge of the child in our midst.

---

Preston Manning is former Leader of the Official Opposition in Parliament and author of *The New Canada* and *Think Big: My Adventures in Life and Democracy*. In 2005 he founded the Manning Centre for Building Democracy. He is a senior fellow with the Fraser Institute and a Companion of the Order of Canada. He lives in Calgary, Alberta.

# As Christmas Comes
~ *Bob Haverluck* ~

As Christmas comes, go where the
cranberry bushes are. In the snow,
dig down past downy, past icy crust,
past grainy to the cranberry leaves
hiding in the grass. Nearby, you will
find a small spruce tree. No higher
than a barbed wire fence. Build a
fire there. Start it with the financial
pages of the newspaper, your pension
printout, and the deed to your house.
Then you will be ready to decorate the tree
with what has been given to be found.
Dress it with the curl of grasses, rosy
leaves of the cranberry, sparrow umber
of dried asters, red berries of the wild
rose ... The final decoration. The blue jay
feather. Now, just sit.
In stillness,

feel yourself being decorated
with thanksgiving.

---

Bob Haverluck is a Winnipeg artist, educator, workshop
leader, writer, and adjunct professor of Theology and Art at
the University of Winnipeg. He has written and illustrated
two books on conflict and peacemaking, *Peace: Perspectives on
Peace / Conflict* and *Love Your Enemies ... And Other Neighbours*.
His drawings have appeared in many publications, including *Harper's Magazine* and *New Statesman*. He has co-written *A
Prairie Mass* with Anne Szumigalski, forthcoming from Coteau
Books in 2009.

# Two Seconds from Death

*~ James A. Taylor ~*

Death is never more than two seconds away on the highway.

At 100 kilometres per hour, it takes less than two seconds to cross a stream of oncoming traffic. To sail off the pavement into a ditch or over a bank. To smash into a rock or a bridge abutment.

I used to know that theoretically. Now I know it from experience.

Joan and I were exploring Newfoundland in a rental car. We were headed west out of St. John's, nearing Gander, the town that became famous for its hospitality to stranded airline passengers on September 11, 2001.

Rain was sluicing down, turning to sleet.

The yellow centre line on the highway had been worn down to an archeological artifact. On rain-slicked pavement, it was almost invisible.

Joan was driving. As we came around a sweeping left-hand curve, we somehow drifted across the centre line into the opposing lane. I looked up from my map into the headlights of an oncoming car.

Joan yanked the wheel back to our side. The car slewed and rocked. When she corrected—probably overcorrected—the car snapped around in the opposite direction and spiralled across two lanes of oncoming traffic.

If we had plowed into a logging truck, even another car, I probably wouldn't be writing this.

But the only thought going through my mind was a sinking feeling that I wasn't looking forward to explaining this incident to the car rental company.

Then we slalomed sideways across the gravel shoulder, ripping both tires on my passenger side off their rims, and into the air.

Anywhere else on that stretch of highway, we would have

rocketed into a rock wall. Or hurtled off an embankment and crashed onto jumbled rocks thirty feet below. Newfoundland isn't called "the Rock" for nothing.

Luckily, we chose the only section with a bank of soft earth rising from the far side of a six-foot-deep drainage ditch.

In slow motion, I watched my window disintegrate into a thousand crystalline fragments and shower into my lap. A great gout of muddy water surged up and fell in on me through where the window had been. And I watched the airbag deflate like a bombastic politician caught in a misdemeanour.

At that point, slow motion ended. A bearded man wrenched Joan's door open and helped her out of the car. "Smoke!" he called, pointing in the direction of the engine.

I couldn't open my door. It was crumpled out of shape, jammed against the bank.

He held Joan's door open for me. I scrambled across.

A young woman was already on her cellphone, calling an ambulance. "I'm a paramedic," she explained, "off-duty."

The bearded man sat us both in the back of his little red Kia, with the heat turned up high. We shivered, shocked. He wrapped his own jacket around Joan.

The ambulance screamed up. Attendants strapped Joan to a body board and immobilized her neck. A friendly cop took statements and arranged to have our car—definitely not drivable—towed into Gander.

The Gander hospital X-rayed Joan's neck and ribs. A nurse found us a local bed and breakfast to stay overnight. The B&B's owner personally drove me to the wrecker's yard, where I recovered our suitcases and other belongings from the battered hulk. The car rental company provided a substitute vehicle without question.

Joan had some major bruises, but nothing broken. I had no injuries at all.

"'Twas the grace of God!" exclaimed several Newfound-
landers, hearing our story.

"Surely God must have saved you for some special purpose," said others.

Maybe. Or maybe not. I don't think God reached down a
divine finger through those rain clouds and cleared oncoming
vehicles out of the way of our spinning car, just so Joan and I
could emerge unscathed.

Why would God do that for us but let others die in hid-
eous pain, crushed in a tangle of tortured metal or barbecued
in a flaming inferno?

I do not believe that God plays favourites that way. Only
arrogance would assume that I matter to God, and others
don't.

Wouldn't it have been a lot easier—and safer for everyone—for God to keep those centre lines painted? To create
tires with better wet-weather traction? To reduce the rainfall a
little? Or to imprint in all of us an instinctive ability to control
dangerous skids?

Devout Christians used to ask Dr. Paul Brand, the famed
missionary surgeon of Vellore, in India, if he had seen any
miracles of healing. Brand usually responded by describing the
medical techniques that gave leprosy victims the use of their
crippled hands again, or that rebuilt eroded noses and ears.

"No, no," his hearers protested, "that's human work. Tell
us what God has done."

"Those are God's miracles," Brand replied. "God uses my
hands."

So I certainly consider it a miracle that Joan and I survived our accident with nothing but bruises. But the miracle
doesn't require divine intervention that violates physics or
biology.

God worked through the engineers who developed seat
belts and airbags, and other engineers who designed cars with

crumple zones to protect occupants. God worked through medical staff who ensured Joan suffered no lasting damage. God worked through other drivers who stopped to help ...

If survival depended only on divine manipulation, then all their efforts were irrelevant. If it were all up to God, it wouldn't matter if we have safer cars, better designed roads, more efficient hospitals ...

So I am profoundly grateful for seat belts and airbags. If we had had that accident forty years ago in our '62 Valiant, without seat belts, airbags, or disk brakes, Joan and I would have been bloody hamburger inside a crumpled metal coffin.

I thank God—and I mean that literally—that there are people who care enough to spend their lives making other people's lives safer.

---

James A. Taylor has written seventeen books, from his first, *An Everyday God* (1981), to the latest, *The Spirituality of Pets* (2007). Although officially retired, he writes two columns a week for Okanagan Valley newspapers and distributes them worldwide by email. He was managing editor of the *United Church Observer* for thirteen years, and founding editor of the clergy journal *PMC* for fifteen. He co-founded the publishing house Wood Lake Books. He lives in Okanagan Centre, British Columbia.

# Elegy for the Red River
~ *Sarah Klassen* ~

Dogs yapping from river properties,
screech of traffic, wind wailing, sucking up the dust.
Biking north I've never heard bells tolling
from this tiny church's miniature tower.
                    Today
there's a funeral. The morning sombre as pewter,
pelicans in black and white procession
heading for the murky river.
                         A century ago
immigrants homesick for the blue Carpathians
built this Orthodox church. Their children's children
trim grass around the graves with cordless whips,
keep the stuccoed walls white, the seven
cupolas burnished.
                      Before the Ukrainian settlers,
Scottish crofters staked out farms along this river
valley where First Nation families for generations
beached their canoes, pitched transient tents,
built fires against the cold and bristling dark,
drummed war. And the Creator's praise.
                        More recently
people like me (Mennonites) are pouring
concrete foundations on choice river lots.
Nostalgic for lost dwellings in another country,
they crave permanence, reprieve from simple living,
travelling the world burdened with material
aid items for Sudan, Darfur, Dominican Republic.
As if they've earned time out from world-repair,
from peace and justice issues, rest
en route to the New Jerusalem. I've observed this
chapel in passing, in fair weather.

One day
because of sudden storm, a punctured tire,
because I've forgotten water or the harsh sun
compels me to reduce speed, I'll stop pumping,
veer off the highway, enter the empty sanctuary,
a stranger in need of shade, relief from traffic,
dogs yapping at my ankles, the unceasing
wind. That day may well be unspectacular.
A host of pelicans heading south or north.
Nothing unusual. An ordinary day
of mercy. Unearned respite for the traveller.
And peace.

---

Sarah Klassen has authored six poetry collections, including *A Curious Beatitude* and *Dangerous Elements*, and two short story collections, *The Peony Season* and *A Feast of Longing*. Her work has appeared in literary magazines across Canada and she has received the Gerald Lampert Memorial Award, the Canadian Authors Association Poetry Award, and the National Magazine Gold Award for poetry. She lives and writes in Winnipeg.

## Words / Tenebrae
~ *Catherine Edward* ~

It was May. Late May and my first extraordinary event. Peter
and Donna Meincke brought me a collection of books-on-tape
to fill the gap because my vision was too blurry to read. How I
enjoyed the books.

I missed being at work. I kept the windows open to let in
the fragrances of May —first lilacs, tilled soil, and such—since
I was living in the Treehouse. But I hadn't figured out how to
answer the phone. First there was the problem of getting the
headpiece off the cradle, which was a real dilemma since my
hands wouldn't cooperate with much of anything and certainly not a slender phone. I'd pick up the entire phone, tip
it upside down and scoop the headpiece up from the bed and
hope the caller was still there so I could say "hello." Saying
"hello" was the hardest. That is a darned difficult word, almost
as bad as linen. I wanted to say "yes!" but it just wasn't me. I
never said "yes!" when I answered the phone. Too self-
conscious. But saying "hello," I know I sounded as if something
was wrong. Drunk.

I had a beastly slur. I could not have imagined that there
is such a string of events that must come into play in order for
words to be delivered properly formed. It is not something
one considers when speech is no trial. I found this the greatest humiliation. Greater than all the rest. That this ability had
deteriorated to the point that I was unhappily self-conscious
with speaking was frustrating in the extreme. I was baffled,
stymied, disconcerted. This really was horrible. Michael
tried to put a positive spin on it, saying that if I sounded like
a drunk, I was an amiable drunk. The problem of the phone
persisted, as during the day I was the only one home, and
there were several things in the offing that needed tending.

When the producer from *Morningside* called, I was un-
nerved, yet there was no way to flee. Could I go to the

Charlottetown CBC studio for a discussion about tax reform
which would give stay-at-home mothers childcare benefits in
line with those of working mothers? Near to my heart, this.

I could not go. I could not talk. I could not drive. I could
not walk. It was obvious I could not talk. On the radio you
want people who can talk. I proposed she [the producer] call
Beverly Smith in Calgary. Beverly would be excellent. And I
apologized for my incapacity and without thinking about the
repercussions I dared to say I had MS and was having a rough
time just then. And since that day I never heard another word
from *Morningside*. Even though three weeks later I could speak
just fine. It never got as bad as that again.

We got another style of telephone with a headpiece,
which is easy to pick up. Beverly was wonderful, and I wrote
to tell her so. But I didn't write any more letters to *Morningside*. There didn't seem any point since, clearly, they had no
further use for me.

I felt no grudge. It was a family misunderstanding. I loved
Peter Gzowski like an old friend. He was my daily companion
through the *This Country in the Morning* and *Morningside* years.
He was present as I reared a family. In the evenings, Michael
would say, "What was Peter up to today?" I hold the CBC in
my affection because it binds a national family together in a
country that makes no sense. Canada is too vast, too diverse
to make sense unless we recognize the reason for it to be is
love: an effort of love is what wills its existence. More than
the national ledger, it is this will that makes Canada. The CBC
is a safe environment for the Canadian family to share its
hopes and dreams, its struggles and triumphs.

One year when we were perched between the last bitter, tired days of winter and the expectant hope of spring,
a particular sharing was taking place across the land. Bill
Richardson, the then host of *RSVP*, read a letter that touched
him so much, he wondered what the rest of us were feeling.

The letter was about a turning point in the life of one ordinary remarkable Canadian. Were there other turning points in other lives? "Please write to me." And we did. Writing is how families stay connected. I wrote, too. This is what Bill read:

## Turning point/Tenebrae

"It is Maundy Thursday. This evening—the Seder, then Tenebrae. Tenebrae ... darkness, shadow. Out of the darkness—light—my turning point.

> I will give thee the treasures of darkness
> And the hidden riches of secret places. (Isaiah 45:3)

"It must be true that life is never quite what it seems, or at least quite what we expect it to be. Certainly not what we demand it to be. The changes and chances of life are most extraordinary when I look at them from the outside, watching.

"Several years ago I was diagnosed with MS. This was not much fun. Frankly, I didn't like this at all. Before, everything was easy. Hands that worked, feet that ran fast, indefatigable energy. Such a fine feeling to be able to accomplish everything! And now? Slow. I am slow. My hands are not the good friends they used to be, my feet have lost their wings, I am weary. How strange, how very strange. Is this me? It feels like I am on the outside, watching.

"There were some moments of sadness, surely a mourning for my lost, vibrant, good health. And yet, that recognized, the depression promised me in all those books never came. I am surrounded by loved ones who clearly see beyond this weariness. It doesn't seem to matter. Not to them for sure, but I want to be a good wife, a helpful mother, and one day to walk in the hemlock forest with grandchildren. Will I always walk in the hemlocks? Where was that depression, and why did it not come?

"When everything was simple, accomplishments flew by unnoticed. Now my days are filled with endless, small tri-

umphs. Everything is a triumph. How remarkable I am! When
I walk I must think about it, but I have thought so well that I
doubt you would notice how hard I am thinking. The garden is
as productive as ever and as beautiful. I made my youngest son
that dreamed-of duffle coat … heavy. It was so heavy I could
just barely handle it. But how handsome it is. There is bread
rising. I have a beautiful ebony walking stick.

"Then Tenebrae came, and I knelt there in the darkness,
wondering. In the darkness everything seemed clear, touch-
able. I felt the treasure in that darkness—the sweet, secret
treasure. And I knew in that moment why I am still so glad
about life … it is not my body, but my soul that is being made
fit. The turning point … from darkness to light. Now, from
the inside, knowing.

> Yet even in the darkness is no darkness with thee,
> But the night is as clear as the day,
> the darkness and the light to thee are both alike.
> (Psalm 139:11)

"Tonight, I will kneel in the darkness of Tenebrae, the
shadow, as we sing Gregorio Allegri's *Miserere Mei* and I will
know, again, the truth. *Deo gratias.*"

---

Catherine Edward lives and writes in rural Prince Edward
Island. She has worked with both CBC Radio and Television,
and as a television current affairs scriptwriter in Charlottetown,
PEI. Her book, *The Brow of Dawn*, won the 2006 PEI Book
Award and was shortlisted as Best Published Atlantic Book in
the 2005 Atlantic Festival. A U.S. edition was released in February 2008 by Bunim & Bannigan Ltd. of New York. She and her
husband have three married children and six grandchildren.

# Jesus Jumps into Bed
~ *Michael Coren* ~

The experience of self-imposed exile. The comfortable émigré, leaving his native country for a privileged alternative. From Britain to Canada. But there is also the pain of distance from loved ones and love. When my mother telephoned me from England, I knew. Just knew. "I've got some bad news for you," she said, beginning to cry. "Dad has had a very bad stroke." I was at the hospital within twenty-four hours.

There he was. Confused, broken, unable to speak. My father, swathed in those pungent, antiseptic hospital odours. Odd how smells provoke memory. I remembered the same smells from when he would wash his hands after work and before dinner, trying to remove the ground-in dirt and oil from his calloused hands.

His skin was always so tough. I can still recall the scraping sound of the razor on his evening stubble, still see the darkness of the water in the basin after he had cleaned his face. Like yesterday, like now.

I would stand next to him as he washed and he would chat away, telling me tales of his own childhood and letting little drops of moral tuition fall into my lap. Simple, and quite marvellous. "A promise is a promise." It was. He never broke one. He was my father.

He drove a black London taxi for more than forty years. It was a job that attracted waves of poor young men after the Second World War, a job that paid a decent wage if you were willing to work a seventy-hour week and not complain or give up.

When I was small and we were driving back from soccer matches, he would sometimes pick up people who were hailing cabs along the way. He wasn't supposed to, not with me there. But I was six or seven and sat in the hollow space next to the driver's seat where the luggage was stored and where he had placed a special little seat. I was barely noticed.

I could never understand why the passengers treated him with such contempt, such patronizing disregard. He was "cabby" and "driver" and "you!" No he wasn't, he was my dad. But he smiled and said nothing and did his job. They weren't good enough to walk in his shadow. I knew that, and he knew I knew that. Which is what really mattered.

And then he told me more stories from his past, such as about the times he boxed for the Royal Air Force. Oh, the pride. And about how his German cousin had gone back to Berlin in the 1930s to rescue his family. The family did not escape and the cousin never came back. A long time ago, said my father, and not for you to worry about. He winked, a wink full of confidence. Never again, he said. I believed him. He was my father.

He always looked so strong, so able to protect me, so powerful. Powerful enough to cry when he felt the need. I heard him weep when my grandmother died. Confusing. How should I react, what should I do? Just be there, as he was for me. He came into my room, saw the fear on my face and recited a short prayer with me for my grandma. He kissed me, held my hand, and then drove me to school before putting in his ten hours. No grumbles, no moans. Of course not. He was my father.

I remember his sheer joy when I went to university, the first in the family to do so. Of course he took too many photographs when I graduated and of course he didn't understand the Latin that was spoken before the meal. Who cares? His wisdom was born long before the Romans imposed their language on the world.

He felt a little out of place, but all that concerned this working man in a smart suit was that his son would not follow in his footsteps. "Do you know why I work such long hours?" he would ask me. "So that you won't have to push a cab around and

tip your hat to everybody." Then he'd pause. "So that you won't
have to." Not said with bitterness but with resolution. There is
dignity in labour, he told me, but shame in sloth.

He didn't come on vacation with us to the English coast
very often, just didn't have the money. He stayed behind, ate
his cheese sandwiches when he got home, and worked. We'd
telephone him and tell him we loved him. He already knew.
When my first child, Daniel, was born, my dad said little.
Just sat and stared and smiled. A circle had been completed,
a story had been told, a great knight had won his battles. He
spoke through his eyes. And what eloquence he had.

What eloquence he still has. As I sit by his bed and hold
his hand, I see the frustration in his eyes. He has, I suppose,
become a child again. The doctors explain that there isn't really very much hope. So we sit and watch and listen and love.
He sits up in his bed, the cuts around his face where he fell
still visible, the IV in his arm, and his eyes nowhere. He wears
those ridiculous hospital pyjamas that are always a size too
small. Oh Dad, what have they done to you?

And then the doors of the ward open. It's my sister,
Stephanie, with her husband, John, and their children, Tessa
and Katie. Three of them walk in, faces grim and grey. But not
all of them. Katie is different. This eight-year-old little girl
doesn't walk in, she skips. In fact she dances, all the way to the
side of her grandpa's bed.

Katie is what is known as handicapped. An odd descrip-
tion really; in my experience, those with the  most moral,
emotional, and spiritual handicaps are the people we generally
regard as being able-bodied. Katie was a very premature baby,
had two strokes herself when she was tiny, and is now, to use
the correct term, "a person with autism."

Katie stands by the bed, and then jumps onto it. In a
British hospital. The country might have changed, but not that
much. This is almost a criminal offence. We say nothing, not

sure of what to do. Then it gets worse. Katie pulls back the blankets and slides inside next to her grandpa.

But Katie hasn't finished yet. She puts her arms around my father, and she falls asleep. We are silent. We just watch. Then ... *then*. For the first time in two days my father shows emotion. Pause. For the first time in more than forty-eight hours my father shows emotion.

He cries.

My father cries. Weeps. Tears bisect his unshaved cheeks and he cries like a baby. We panic like babies. We call for the doctor, shout for the nurses. This wasn't meant to happen. What is going on here? The doctor arrives and, bless him, he didn't mean to say what he did. "Oh my, I didn't expect this. What happened? This is miraculous!"

He was right. It was. A miracle had taken place. Not performed by me or any of the other educated, respected people in that hospital, not by anyone with a theological degree or medical training. But by a little girl whose parents had been advised to leave their church because "Katie is a bit noisy for some of the people here."

Katie performed a miracle that day. In fact, Katie was Jesus Christ that day. She gave the gift of unconditional love. She didn't judge the situation, judge the person, judge anything. She reached out in love, of love, with love. We with our university degrees, polished manners, and social acceptance fumbled around looking for answers. Katie didn't even have to ask the question. She merely lived the example of Jesus.

I didn't fly three thousand miles in the middle of the night because I feared my father and wanted to obey him, or because I thought that the law demanded it. I did so because I loved him. In the same way, I hope, I do my best to live according to God's will, not because I fear God but because I love God. This is something that Katie knows very well. Pray all of us will listen to her teaching.

Michael Coren hosts the nightly *Michael Coren Show* on CTS television and co-hosts a daily radio show on CFRB called *Two Bald Guys with Strong Opinions*. He writes a weekly column for the Toronto, Ottawa, Calgary, Edmonton, and Winnipeg *Sun* newspapers and the *London Free Press*. He also writes for *Catholic Insight*, *Women's Post*, the *Interim*, and the *National Post*. He is the author of eleven books, including biographies of G.K. Chesterton, C.S. Lewis, and J.R.R. Tolkien.

# Kissing Mother Oksana
~ *Katya Szalasznyj* ~

When our daughter Anastasia was three and our son Alexander almost eight, Alex went away for a week. He had never been away this long before. We heard nothing from him, so we assumed he was all right, being at his uncle's with his cousins. But his absence played on Anastasia's heart. As we were driving to pick him up, she said, out of the blue, "When I see him, I will kiss his arm." And sure enough, as soon as we arrived, she jumped out of the van, ran straight for Alex, and kissed his arm.

Observers have noted, "That's what those Orthodox are always doing—kissing!" There is the thrice-holy kiss upon greeting and kissing exchanged at the altar. There is the kiss of peace in the Divine Liturgy. And bread, accidentally dropped on the floor, is picked up and kissed.

We are here to kiss the memory of a woman who was, in many respects, a spiritual mother to us. Oksana Olekshy was born in the province of Volhynia in Ukraine during the Second World War. She sometimes told how as a baby she was thrown from a train, to which she attributed her migraine headaches. Along with her two sisters and a somewhat extended family, she was raised in the Orthodox community of Winnipeg's North End, surrounded by the music, literature, languages, and colours of immigrant life.

She became an interior design student, an opera singer, and eventually a priest's wife, mother of Ilaria, and parish mother of dozens in a fledgling Saskatoon congregation, Holy Resurrection. In Orthodox language her role has many names—a Presbytera, Dobrodika, Matushka, Kyrie, Proestesa. She was the mother of our parish for thirty years, the oft-uncelebrated helper, and the soother of many anxieties. Herself a sketcher and painter, affirmation of personhood and love of beauty were etched on the walls of her life.

*1974.* In a house containing an endless array of books, plants, and art, Oksana is filling a coffee pot and chatting with the young students who have filled the parsonage mid-week. It is fall in a university town full of lonely, displaced, anxious students from all parts of the province.

Auburn-haired with chiselled cheekbones and solemn dark eyes, Oksana is dressed in a gold sweater and a long skirt in fall plaids. A cascade of amber at her neckline catches the candlelight of the dining room. A hint of classical music pours from a radio among the cookbooks.

Oksana has worked all day in the campus library and is fatigued. One must bend a little to hear her, catching the faint scent of fine cologne. A quiet dignity and beauty come from this woman. She chats engagingly about the plant by the sink and the need to soak it well once in a while, and how beautifully it blooms. Her hands lift a stack of cups and cut a cake, as she talks all the while to those beside her. She accepts their being there. There is no why-are-you-here look.

The music and the conversation from the living room become louder. Oksana has quietly gone off and joined her daughter, who sits colouring at one corner of the dining-room table. Now she is immersed in the choice of colours, the shapes and lines in the book before them.

*1980.* Oksana sits near the back of the church. The service has ended. The light of noonday plays upon the double strand of pearls around her neck and the pearl, coral, and turquoise brooch on the lapel of her jacket.

Pausing to answer a question, she reaches into a grey purse by her side. It is a veritable treasure bag of everything. It contains a sketchbook and a book of poetry in which are tucked some greeting cards of still-life flowers. There is the devotional *Bread of Life* that she is fond of reading, book-marked by paper icons and little notes that she has writ-

ten—so many things that now the book is bound with an
elastic band. Then there's candy for the children of the parish,
lozenges for sore throats, always a package of Kleenex should
anyone have a tear— all of those items that somehow can
make up the reaches of that mysterious phenomenon called "a
purse." Did I mention a screwdriver? Then there's a pen that
is also a flashlight, except a minute later, she's given it to a
child who has been staring at it. "Here, it's yours," she says. A
mother's purse, full of things—a symbol of her relating, her
giving. Her purse is *her*.

Strangely, this Great Grey Bag has no overtones of
finance, as she is the world's greatest non-shopper, ordering
even toiletry items from the catalogue to avoid the hassle of
shopping. It reflects the fullness of her life. And it is full! She
jokes that the sheer weight of it would be enough to injure
anyone who ever tried to block her path.

*1983.* Morning at the Olekshy home on Eighteenth Street.
Sounds of scurrying bring Oksana around a corner, where she
meets a frightened young man who has just broken into their
home. He leaps at the open window, rushing out as fast as he
can. "Don't hurry so much, you'll hurt yourself!" she calls to
him in genuine concern, as his back disappears. She reminds us
of the father of St. Siluoan the Athonite who, upon stumbling
upon a thief helping himself, promptly hid himself lest the thief
should be embarrassed being caught in the act of his sin.

At hand is not fear and violation of property, but the protection of the dignity of another, of keeping the vision of real
life. You would not hear this story from her, for she is not one
to talk about herself.

*1989.* We drive up to find Oksana in her garden, snipping
off dead leaves, making way for new life. By now, bouts of ill
health are more common, and she is not outdoors much

anymore. She is wearing a cream straw hat with a sweeping brim and an attached polka-dotted scarf, dressing for the occasion as one who loves life and finds it on her own patch of ground. How many of us visit her every spring and leave with boxes of bits, knobs, and roots of perennials—iris, ranunculus, daisies, johnny-jumps, peonies, and wild violets.

Hers is a sharing garden, a place of joy. As Mother Maria of Normanby writes, she works "repentance on her patch of ground." In a similar way, the church is a garden to her. Seeing the beauty of other people's children, she is as apt to sketch a child as she might a flower.

*1997.* Sounds of sterile machines jar the stark silence. The night seems to last forever, but then it finally passes in palliative care at St. Paul's Hospital. Sunrise at this time of year comes at about ten after six through the tall windows facing the east. I watch the quiet, apricot rays of sun upon her face as they turn to gold. Her attention is riveted on the glowing horizon, caught in the unique beauty of this unfolding sunrise. She is oblivious to her surroundings, and to me. Even to her pain. It is voyeuristic of me to observe her oneness with this living, dawning day, so I turn away. She is at prayer, facing east in the Orthodox way.

*Today.* Oksana has not left us. We remember how, over the years, she showed and did not tell how to live and how to die. Her life spoke of an uncommon integration of physical and spiritual giving, in that blend defined so curiously by Dostoyevsky: "We go from such faith to such pancakes!" From her spiritual devotion to her flowers and her sweets for children, from her quiet love to her sketches left behind, all parts of her life were seamless, living out the Orthodox understanding of sanctification of the physical through Christ's incarnation.

A prominent Greek father, Hierotheos Vlachos, writes, "A visitor to the monasteries of the Holy Mountain will discover that the greatest compliment one can receive from the monks is to be invited to kiss the holy relics ... They are the cell's greatest possession and blessing." In this way, we also kiss the memory of Mother Oksana. We remember her in the *proskomedia*, the preparation of the Holy Communion cup. We sing "Memory Eternal" for her and hold an annual lecture in her honour.

Especially, we pause by Mother Oksana's grave. We sing "Christ Is Risen" and bless her grave with holy water. And the prairie sun illumines the words etched on the smooth black granite of her stone: "She walked lightly on the face of the earth."

---

Katya Szalasznyj grew up in the Good Spirit Lake district of Saskatchewan, an enclave of colourful Slavic settlement. Her rural life there was central to her development as a writer and archivist. She and her husband, Vasil, are founding members of Holy Resurrection Orthodox Church, Saskatoon. She is the archivist for the Archdiocese of Canada, Orthodox Church in America, and is a member of the History and Archives Committee and the Canonization Commission of the OCA.

Glimpses of Glory

# Remembering World Youth Day 2002
*~ Thomas Rosica ~*

In July 2002, Toronto hosted the 17th International World Youth Day. Several hundred thousand young people from 172 nations descended upon the city—and with them came the elderly and infirm Pope John Paul II. To kick off the event on July 23, the pope defied all odds and stunned all critics when he painstakingly walked down the steps of that Alitalia plane at Pearson International Airport instead of using the special lift prepared for him.

To the government officials gathered at the airport and to the people of Canada, the pope spoke these words: "Canadians are heirs to an extraordinarily rich humanism, enriched even more by the blend of many different cultural elements ... In a world of great social and ethical strains, and confusion about the very purpose of life, Canadians have an incomparable treasure to contribute—on condition that they preserve what is deep, and good, and valid in their own heritage."

Toronto may have lost the Olympic bid two years earlier, but it struck gold with World Youth Day, which I was privileged to serve as its national director. The sheer numbers of people taking part in the four days of events astounded us. More than 350,000 people packed Exhibition Place on Thursday afternoon, July 25, for the opening ceremony with Pope John Paul II.

The following evening, Toronto's majestic University Avenue was transformed into the Via Dolorosa of Jerusalem as more than half a million people took part in the ancient Stations of the Cross. The CBC/Radio-Canada told us that the worldwide television audience that night was more than a billion people in 160 countries.

The deeply moving Saturday evening candlelight vigil at Downsview Park drew together more than 600,000 people, and the concluding papal Mass on Sunday, with its atmospheric theatrics, gathered 850,000 people at a former military base. Even the most cynical among us could not help but be impressed, even moved, by the streams of young people who expressed their joy at being Christians in a complex and war-torn world.

On the tarmac that Saturday evening of the vigil, John Paul II spoke to the young people. "The new millennium opened with two contrasting scenarios," he declared. "One, the sight of multitudes of pilgrims coming to Rome during the Great Jubilee to pass through the Holy Door which is Christ, our Saviour and Redeemer; and the other, the terrible terrorist attack on New York, an image that is a sort of icon of a world in which hostility and hatred seem to prevail. The question that arises is dramatic: On what foundations must we build the new historical era that is emerging from the great transformations of the twentieth century? Is it enough to rely on the technological revolution now taking place, which seems to respond only to criteria of productivity and efficiency, without reference to the individual's spiritual dimension or to any universally shared ethical values? Is it right to be content with provisional answers to the ultimate questions, and to abandon life to the impulses of instinct, to short-lived sensations or passing fads?"

The provocative images the pope evoked that night remain engraved on people's memories. Terrorism, along with ethnic and religious divisions, generates violence that seems to have no end. Economic insecurity raises collective anxieties. And against that backdrop, we heard our challenge—to recover the depth, beauty, and vastness of the church's mission.

## Papal pedagogy

Pope John Paul II had a particular fascination for and effective ministry among young people. The two largest recorded crowds in history have been for World Youth Day Masses in Manila (1995) and Rome (2000). In the midst of those great gatherings and the hundreds of meetings with young people, the pontiff left us a pedagogy, a way of meeting and accompanying the young along the journey. One of the hallmarks of John Paul

II's interaction with young people was that he called them his "young friends." And he meant it. As we observed that summer in Toronto, he enjoyed the company of youth.

*Challenge* was one of John Paul II's favourite terms. During World Youth Day, he challenged young people to be "brave," "strong," and to "have courage." He saw in the valour of so many of his own contemporaries during World War II the capacity of young people for bravery, courage, and heroism.

His parting words from the Downsview Park stage still resound in my ears: "You are young, and the pope is old; eighty-two or eighty-three years of life is not the same as twenty-two or twenty-three. But the pope still fully identifies with your hopes and aspirations. Although I have lived through much darkness, under harsh totalitarian regimes, I have seen enough evidence to be unshakably convinced that no difficulty, no fear is so great that it can completely suffocate the hope that springs eternal in the hearts of the young. You are our hope, the young are our hope. Do not let that hope die! Stake your lives on it! We are not the sum of our weaknesses and failures; we are the sum of the Father's love for us and our real capacity to become the image of his Son."

The experiences of World Youth Days in recent years have brought much new life to each of the countries where these events have taken place. Now, several years after the great event of Toronto 2002, we need to take stock of the gifts we received, asking how the vision and hope of John Paul II have impacted our own efforts in pastoral ministry with young people.

### What we learned

What have the joy, exuberance, and creativity surrounding the 2002 World Youth Day taught us, and how have they transformed youth and young adult ministry in the Canadian church? How have we initiated a "preferential option" for young people in the church today? How can we give the flavour of the gospel and the light of Christ to the world?

One of the important goals of World Youth Day is to instill hope and vibrancy in the church—to differ with the cynicism, despair, and meaninglessness so prevalent in the world today. John Paul II knew well that our world today offers fragmentation, loneliness, alienation, and rampant globalization that exploits the poor.

In recent years we have witnessed a phenomenon that our current Pope Benedict XVI has called "a dictatorship of relativism"—the deconstruction of all objectivity in our perceptions of reality. We have witnessed the crisis of marriage and family life. We see the loss of respect for human life and human dignity. We are living through the results of a serious crisis of fatherhood in our contemporary world.

The preparation for World Youth Day 2002 offered the church in Canada some unique and profound moments to deepen our Christian devotion. Many Canadians are unlikely to forget the powerful images of the World Youth Day Cross on its historic 43,000-kilometre pilgrimage through more than 350 cities, towns, and villages—from sea to sea to sea.

The presentation of the Stations of the Cross on Friday evening, July 26, 2002, was a provocative and profound witness of the Christian story in the heart of a modern city. How have we continued this tradition in our parish communities and youth activities? Do we acknowledge the need for solid, biblically rooted Christian piety and devotion in the lives of young people today?

During his pontificate, Pope John Paul II proclaimed 482 saints and 1,338 blesseds ("blessed" is the last step before being declared a saint). Young adults need heroes and heroines today, and the Pope gave us outstanding models of holiness and humanity at each World Youth Day, especially ours in Canada. The saints and blessed ones remind us that on the path to heaven, we are never finished; we are only and always on the way. When we think of holiness in these terms—as a kind of direction, rather than a destination—we have a sense that what unites us with the saints, our fellow travellers, is much deeper than all that sets us apart.

John Paul II summed up the whole mission as follows: "Meet Christ; become friends with him; announce to others the miracle of his love!" His strategy and pedagogy with young people was endless patience, loving closeness, and a bold call to be saints.

The theme of Canada's 2002 World Youth Day was "You are the salt of the earth. You are the light of the world," taken from Matthew's Gospel, chapter 5. This theme served as a leitmotiv during the buildup to World Youth Day 2002, for the event itself, and in the follow-up in local churches throughout the world. It also inspired the establishment of Canada's first national Catholic television network, Salt and Light Television, which I was asked to direct in 2003.

During World Youth Days, bishops and cardinals serve as teachers and catechists. Thousands of young people gather around them to hear reflections based on the Word of God, and in particular on the theme of the event. This novel invention has taken on a life of its own, becoming an intrinsic part of the celebrations. The teaching sessions have become not only a unique encounter between generations, but also an opportunity to proclaim and preach the Word of God across cultures, offering to young people concrete possibilities for living a biblically rooted life.

In Toronto, we saw another unique gift of John Paul II: fatherhood. In *Radiation of Fatherhood*, the 1964 drama he wrote when he was still Polish Bishop Karol Wojtyla, he suggested that becoming a father meant being "conquered by love," which liberates us from the false freedom of self-absorption. For millions of young people worldwide, the pope's spiritual fatherhood was a reflection of the fatherhood of God. I'm convinced that the young people responded to him so positively because in many cases he was the father they never had and the grandfather they never knew.

During the celebrations of 2002, John Paul II offered us powerful opportunities to become bearers of hope, agents of community, neighbours to those around us, and instruments of a moral globalization that must accompany all other globalization efforts. He challenged us to give a reason for the hope we have to the people we meet each day. John Paul II taught us that if we wish to be convincing in our apology for the faith, we must first be convinced about the faith.

## Boldness and solidarity

As we think further about John Paul II's call to the transformation of Canadian culture and to deeply Christian roots, two key words come to mind: boldness and solidarity. They come out of the strategy of the early church, as seen in Luke's Gospel and the Acts of the Apostles.

In Acts 4, Peter and John were arrested and brought before the officials. They were interrogated, threatened, and ordered to speak no longer in the name of Jesus the Lord. Once they were released, their community uttered a remarkable prayer. It wasn't about the actual harm inflicted on the believers but about the fact that the Word of God was chained, threatened, and suffocated.

The community prayed for guidance. It wanted to understand the events in the light of faith, to discover the meaning of what had happened. When they had prayed, we read, the place in which they were gathered was shaken and they were all filled with the Holy Spirit and spoke the Word with boldness.

Then in Acts 18 we see the apostle Paul facing hostility in Corinth. The Lord responds in a vision: "Do not be afraid; keep on speaking, do not be silent. For I am with you, and no one is going to attack and harm you, because I have many people in this city." So Paul stayed for a year and a half, teaching the people the Word of God. What a wonderful encouragement this is—that we not despair. We are not alone. God has many friends with whom we can develop prayerful networks of solidarity and friendship.

World Youth Day in Canada woke us up, infused us with joy, and reminded us of our gifts. It reminded us of the qualities of hospitality, tolerance, and peacemaking that have characterized this nation. It called us back to our deeply Christian origins and heritage. As we bask in the radiant memories of the summer of 2002, we can admit now that it was no panacea or quick fix to the problems facing us today. It was not a show, a rave party, a protest, or photo opportunity. It was an invitation. Against a global background of terror and fear, economic collapse in many countries, and ecclesial scandals, World Youth Day 2002 presented a bold, alternative vision of compelling beauty, hope, and joy. This gives us courage and solidarity to help future generations.

---

Father Thomas Rosica, CSB, was National Director of World Youth Day 2002 and currently serves as Chief Executive Officer of the Salt and Light Catholic Media Foundation and Television Network. A noted Scripture scholar and author, he has lectured widely and worked in interfaith relations in Canada since 1989. From 1994 to 2000, he was the Executive Director and Pastor of the Newman Centre Catholic Mission at the University of Toronto. He resides in Toronto.

# No Hurry in L'Arche

~ *Carolyn Whitney-Brown* ~

Geoff was skipping up and down the living room with Helen, together singing a spontaneous sheet-folding song. Geoff was my husband of eight years. Helen was an older woman with Down's Syndrome who combined a righteous dignity with a playful sense of humour. She was one of the early members of the well-established L'Arche Daybreak community in Richmond Hill, Ontario, and we had just moved into a house with Helen. She had a long history of welcoming new people and helping them feel at home. I hadn't seen my beloved husband so ridiculous in several years. I couldn't take my eyes off them.

L'Arche, an international federation of communities where people with intellectual disabilities and their assistants live together, began in 1964 when Jean Vanier, son of Governor General Georges Vanier and Pauline Vanier, invited two men to move out of their institution and live with him in a house. Although the first house was in France, it was a particularly Canadian endeavour. Canadians like small projects with global significance and wide-ranging influence. In forty-four years, L'Arche has touched thousands of lives worldwide and now has 132 communities in thirty-five countries.

Geoff and I had been on a long exploration together. We had met through Inter-Varsity Christian Fellowship at the University of Toronto. We each had histories of leadership. By the time Geoff was cavorting with Helen, we had completed PhDs in English literature.

In 1984, when a friend's brother died of a brain tumour, my friend had confided that he "didn't want to forget how to walk with those who walk more slowly." The words stayed with me as Geoff and I pursued our doctorates, learning to run with the intellectually fastest. Gradually, we recognized that we found the most joy and life not in our successful academic projects, but in the time we had spent with people on the margins. I had worked

with people with intellectual disabilities in Ottawa and with
independent women in wheelchairs in Toronto. Together we had
made close friends at a soup kitchen in Rhode Island, then at a
preschool for underprivileged children in the United Kingdom.
We actively participated in the peace movement.

Several intentional communities in Britain welcomed us into
their lives and history. At the end of that year, a friend invited us
to spend six months in Kenya. "You are really community people
but you don't understand community until you live in Africa!" he
insisted. "COME!" he wrote in inch-high letters, on behalf of the
Brothers of Mercy. Like Peter when Jesus invited him to get out
of the boat, we jumped at the invitation.

During our time in Kenya and an extended visit to war-torn
Ethiopia, we learned that visitors are a blessing. *Hakuna metata*,
said often, meant "No problem." It did not mean no worries, as the
Lion King would later translate it. It meant, "If you need something, I'm here for you, as you will be for me. We are in it together, so your request is no problem." We learned never to refuse a
gift. We also learned about riots, pepper spray, brutal poverty, and
slum clearance. We soaked up lessons in playfulness in a country
where more than half the population is younger than fifteen. In
Africa, there was music, rhythm, joy, energy, and no hurry.

And to the delight of our African friends, we found we were
pregnant! "What are you going to do?" people asked. In Kenya
we said, "Have a baby, become parents, maybe become ancestors!" and everyone was happy for us. In Canada the same answer
got concern. "Yes," would be the response, with wrinkled brow,
"but what are you going to *do*?"

## Life in L'Arche

In England, we had visited a L'Arche house called Bethany in
Bognor Regis for several days. A chaotic, intense, painful, and
hilarious spirit captivated us, and on our last evening, one of the
men read about Martha and Mary and Lazarus from a book of

Gospel stories by Jean Vanier. "Jesus loves them very much," he read slowly, "he often goes to their home to rest." We could see why Jesus would like to rest in L'Arche.

Back in Canada, we went for lunch with Henri Nouwen who, like ourselves, was a recovering academic in search of a home. "You are not kids trying to find yourselves," Henri mused. "Your lives are very directed."

So we moved into a Daybreak house with Helen, George, Anne-Marie, Gordie, and several assistants. In the way of L'Arche, almost immediately the head of house went on a retreat, and we were left in charge, bewildered by our sudden responsibility and by pages of complex instructions regarding dietary restrictions, behaviour, and consequences.

It could have seemed daunting, but really it was just a matter of living together. We cooked, washed, made mistakes, forgave each other, played, sang, went for walks, did laundry. And Geoff and Helen folded sheets.

Thus we rapidly learned the most important thing: celebration is essential to any shared life. Jean Vanier observes that forgiveness and celebration are at the heart of community, because these are two faces of love: "Celebration nourishes us, restores hope, and brings us the strength to live with the suffering and difficulties of everyday life."

After a month or so, it struck me. "Our lives are like that parable!" I announced to Geoff. "You know, the one where the rich people don't want to come to the banquet, so the host welcomes the poor and homeless and all who wouldn't normally be invited to the banquet. That's what L'Arche is doing." I was tired from cooking and was trying to feel noble by spiritualizing my activity. "Yup," my wiser husband replied, "we had no home and we got invited!"

In some ways, our seven years in L'Arche are a big blur. I was pregnant or breastfeeding for all but six months. I suffered through a postpartum depression. As with all parents of young children, many nights featured less than a full night's sleep. In a large community of more than a hundred people, there were endless crises, emergencies, requests for support. It was beautiful—and relentless.

In other ways, our Daybreak years are some of the most vivid of my life. As our Jesuit friend Doug McCarthy has suggested, when we are most alive, we have stories to tell. Those years were surely alive!

For several of those years, we chose to spend Christmas with the community so that there would be children at the Christmas dinner. In 1993 we stayed because we couldn't go far. We were expecting our second child in early January. Soon after her birth, Monica was diagnosed with pulmonary stenosis, a heart defect that would require surgery within a week.

In times like this, community life shines. We were wrapped in love. Members of the community who did not express themselves in words stroked Monica's head and hugged us close. L'Arche believes that the way to peace is to hold the weakest and most vulnerable members at the centre. In those days, the weakest member of Daybreak was Monica, and our community united around our tiny daughter. L'Arche communities all over the world prayed for us. A friend asked people at the retreat he was leading to pray for us. Exhausted, postpartum, scared, we rested in the great net of love and support, grateful that we didn't have to depend on only our own faith and strength.

The day Monica was to go into hospital, Henri called everyone at morning Mass to gather and lay hands on her weak little body and on Geoff and me as we held her. It was a powerful prayer. The very cells of our bodies soaked up the love and support of our community. Monica's successful surgery and life remains a continuing source of wonder and gratitude for all of us.

This practice of blessing someone by gathering close to place a hand on them was something we learned in L'Arche. Jean Vanier often says that L'Arche is founded on the body. We learned to bless physically, not just through words.

Deaths in the community were likewise body-events. The day Helen died, I went to see her in the hospital with her old friend and housemate, George. When we lived together, they could easily drive each other crazy. George needed a nightlight on in the hall; Helen would unplug it and take it to her room. George wanted the stair light on; Helen would turn it off, over and over through the day. George was a big man with enormous hands that were red and often a bit swollen. Helen was a tiny woman with extremely small hands. They had known each other for decades.

On that last afternoon, George and I sat by Helen's bed, and Helen held one of George's fingers. More than held it—she clung to it, her tiny hand slowly turning blue as her body's oxygen grew insufficient, clutching George's big, red hand. So they sat, the hands that turned lights on and off, now holding each other in silence, the little blue hand, the big red hand. The moment summed up community life for me.

A few days later, we walked into the funeral home and were greeted by the well-dressed funeral director with his gentle voice. "And where may I direct you?" Bellows of laughter could be heard echoing down one of the carpeted hallways. "Probably down there!" we suggested. At Daybreak wakes and funerals, caskets were open. We touched our dead friends, patted their folded hands, ruffled their hair, adjusted their glasses, tucked notes and photos in with them. We would gather in a big circle around the casket every hour or so and sing a song or hymn, cry and laugh, and tell some stories. When Henri Nouwen died, we made him a casket at the Daybreak woodworking studio and kept prayerful vigil with his body through the night.

Through those years, Geoff and I and our three children visited twenty L'Arche communities in Canada, Europe, and Honduras. Each community was different, but each felt like home. What did we learn? Overall, we confirmed what we had learned in Africa. No hurry in L'Arche. Visitors are a blessing. *Hakuna metata.*

L'Arche deepened our understanding of spirituality and of liturgical celebration. L'Arche spirituality is down-to-earth. Some L'Arche houses have prayers at the table after meals, while others gather in the evening to share about their days and offer themselves and each other to God. It is not as formal as prayer in a vowed religious community, and people are free to participate or not, as they choose. We incorporated that rhythm and freedom into our family life.

Daybreak also had a chapel where the community and friends gathered to pray. It had chairs around the perimeter, but everyone who was able sat on the thick carpet. Like an African bus, everyone crammed in, and there was always room for more. It was intimate and cozy. We learned that worship space can be simple. Any box with a beautiful bit of cloth and a candle could become the centre point gathering people in prayer. L'Arche communities are generally not wealthy; most have simple worship spaces. Flowers, cloths, candles, and icons can create a sacred space almost anywhere.

Early on, I confided in someone that I was enjoying Mass and community worship and celebrations more than I was enjoying the daily life with others. He pointed out that my appreciation of these communal times was rooted in our life together. He was right. After we left Daybreak, I sometimes enjoyed joining the community's events, but without the shared life, some of the richness was gone.

## Afterword

Once when Jean Vanier was visiting, one of the long-term members of the community asked him, "So many people come and live with us, and then they leave and I get very sad. What should I do?" Jean's answer was immediate. "That is your vocation, to form people in love and send them out. That is your mission."

Too soon we were declared formed and ready to be sent out. We had a grand goodbye party. Everyone came in African dress, did silly skits and songs about us, made speeches, gave us a wonderful present, and we all danced.

We moved to Toronto, near siblings and cousins. It was a relief to be with more people in our stage of life. At Daybreak, a revered nun shook her head at our mess of toys and piles of unfolded clean laundry and told us we really weren't making it. We were stricken. But in our new neighbourhood, our kids rapidly made friends and all their houses looked that way! We were grateful to be normalized.

Still, we missed our community. Church seemed too quiet without some random verbal expressions and lots of coming and going. We didn't want to forget how to walk with those who walked more slowly. As a family we volunteered at a derelict local nursing home that welcomed people with little or no income, and we met some extraordinary people.

In L'Arche, the first place of belonging, celebration, peacemaking, and community building is in each household. In a culture where home is often taken for granted and real work begins outside, we have worked at building our family community. Each evening, we continue to gather around a candle to share about our day and to pray. Often, we welcome others into our family circle.

We had learned deep truths about suffering in L'Arche, both others' and our own. Leaving the Daybreak community after seven years felt like we had wrenched out part of our hearts. Jean Vanier wrote to us, saying that he was thinking of the Emmaus passage, where Jesus comes to walk with the heartbroken disciples and says, "Didn't you know that the Christ had to suffer to enter his glory?" Over and over in our lives, we reflected, we make choices for risk or renewal, and those often require letting go of something comfortable. Letting go with gratitude—even of people and things and places we have loved—is a basic life skill.

In their early days, many L'Arche communities and friends went on pilgrimages together. "Journeys and celebrations are

so important," writes Jean Vanier, "for opening up our hearts
and minds to other realities, for breaking up the routines of our
everyday life." Maybe our L'Arche years were part of our choice
in 2003 to travel, learning to love the earth and all its creatures
anew. We learned a lot travelling around North America for thirteen months. But that is another story ...

Carolyn Whitney-Brown and her family were part of the L'Arche
Daybreak community in Ontario from 1990 to 1997. Following
L'Arche, she taught Religious Studies at St. Jerome's University
in Waterloo, Continuing Education at St. Michael's College in
Toronto, and coordinated national projects for the Canadian
Council of Churches, the Evangelical Fellowship of Canada,
and the United Church of Canada. Carolyn recently edited the
volume *Jean Vanier: The Essential Writings*. The Whitney-Browns live
on Vancouver Island.

# The Day My Father Was Born Again, Again

~ *Maxine Hancock* ~

It is only after the funeral, when fatigue washes over me, that I recognize the magnitude of what has happened. I have been this tired only four times in my life before, each time after having given every grain of emotional energy and physical endurance to birthing a human person into new life. The fatigue tells me that attending to my father's death has been something of that magnitude. This time, though, I was midwife to a birthing, joining in a groaning travail known to all creation … as my father was born again, again.

My father had been "born again" at age nineteen. All his long life, he loved to tell how he had started to attend meetings at the Gospel Hall in Calgary with his best friend, Walt Bennett. Convinced by the preaching of the Word that Jesus Christ had a legitimate claim on his life, he decided one Sunday that the next Sunday he would ask Jesus to be his personal Saviour. That long week he counted the cost and the next Sunday, he stayed after the gospel preaching of the evening service to give his life unreservedly to Jesus Christ.

"I didn't jump over any fences or shout 'Hallelujah,'" he would always explain, "but I had made a business deal with God: I had given Christ my life and accepted his offer of eternal life, and I knew that for me everything had changed. I had been born again."

This summer, seventy years later, the outcome of that faith reached its climax at the point of his crossing over from one life to another. The process was as mysterious as his first "new birth," as much a matter of faith in God's Word. This time, I was there.

Please don't think it was easy, or pretty, although as dying goes I suppose it was routine. Emergency surgery on a depleted and aged body, complications, death. It is, for me, the sightlessness of his eyes that is the strongest memory when I stop trying not to think about it.

My sister Marg and I keep watch on each side of his bed: two middle-aged women made one by shared love and grief. We speak softly to him: "We're here with you, Dad," we say. "You can go now, it's time to go now. We bless you on your way, Dad. You can go home, Dad." We cannot stop crying, and yet what we feel is joy as much as sadness.

I had cut short a trip in the United Kingdom when the surgeon asked Marg to relay a message: "Tell your sister if she wants to see her dad before he dies, she'd better get on the plane now." (I do not think I need to see my dad—we have said goodbyes before I left Canada; but I do feel I need to be with my sister and help our mother.) I cancelled everything and came home, across an ocean, across a continent.

It is only when we are delayed four hours before taking the short flight from Calgary to Edmonton that I know why I have had to come home: not for them, but for me. My heart cries louder with each passing hour as we await takeoff between encircling thunderstorms, "Oh Dad, I'm coming. Wait for me, Dad ... I'm coming to see you home."

When at last we lift out of Calgary, I look through the bevelled squares of the plane windows at the white and blue stencilling of his beloved Rockies, and I say goodbye for him: goodbye, blue mountains; goodbye, summer green prairie, gold under the long fingers of the late afternoon sun; goodbye, beautiful, beautiful earth.

Dad knows me immediately, and through the hallucinations that the pain medication induces, he shapes the question, "Is there some cause for alarm?" I talk with the doctor about changing pain control so Dad is more lucid; and when the almost-inevitable pneumonia develops, we ask for a family conference with the surgeon. Please, we say, don't treat the pneumonia. Let this be his last struggle. Let him go.

But, even then, how that shrunken body clings to life. We are with Dad as much as we can be. We stay at a hostel provided by the Rotary club, halfway between the long-term care hospital where our mother is and the hospital where our father lingers, two minutes from a call from nursing staff at either place.

Over the next few days, people keep coming in to say goodbye to Dad, to say thank you. Sometimes he squeezes a hand, knows who is there, mouths a comment, even prays for them. Sometimes he is too far away to know or respond. My father and mother have lived, simply and hospitably, in a sequence of modest homes in various cities in Alberta for the more than sixty-five years of their marriage. Yet the people who say goodbye are from around the globe, with names from Jones and Mathison to Oostra and Khan and Tran, and from four generations. Walt Bennett, his boyhood chum and spiritual mentor, comes and sits a while every day right down to the last one, when he says, simply, "Goodbye, Buddy. I'll be seeing you."

One evening near the end, my father is clear enough to talk with me through the "evening shift."

"I think I'll be going home to the Lord tonight," he says.

I nod. "Maybe you will, Dad." I think: Is he asking me to have someone come in and pray with him? So I ask, "Is that all right?"

"Why, of course!" he replies without hesitation, surprised that I should ask such a question. It is well with his soul.

The staff puts a cot in the room for us as we take turns staying overnight, close enough to be at Dad's side when he speaks or calls out, but able to get a bit of sleep. We sing, those nights, quietly, the old hymns and choruses he used to sing or whistle. When he is conscious, Dad mouths the words along with us: "Oh, that will be / Glory for me ..." and "Face to face with Christ my Saviour ..." Sometimes he smiles as the notes fade into the twilight around us.

❧

The last night of his life it is my turn to sleep on the cot, to be the physical presence of love and family in his room. After a couple of days in which he has been unresponsive or unable to make himself understood, there is a small miracle: this night, I can understand everything he says.

"I'm here with you, Dad," I say, and he murmurs, "Still here, sweetheart?" We sleep in fits and starts, both coughing in the dry air, a sort of secret conversation of throat clearings and coughs.

At about two in the morning, Dad is suddenly awake. "Oh," he cries out, "I'm so cold."

This is it, I think.

I ask for a warmed blanket and the night nurses bring it and pack it carefully in around him. The warmth spreads through him and we sleep again.

At about four he begins to whimper. Like a child. Like a hurt puppy. This time the nurses and I are just able to understand him: "My right leg is hurting almost unbearably." Much more than competent, the nurses are wonderfully gentle and kind. They usher me out of the room, suggesting I go for coffee. The first light of the day is streaking the sky with mauve as they turn him, make him comfortable, sedate him again, and sit with him until he is quiet.

By the next morning, he no longer responds. His hand is relaxed and unflexed, the grip gone. Near suppertime, Marg and I can see that his breathing has changed, become shallower. Now just the minute-to-minute reality of the last hour of our dad's life, the rasping of his breathing. In and out. In and out.

We ask Marg's husband to read from Dad's Bible the passage we choose: "The time has come for my departure. I have fought the good fight, I have finished the race, I have kept the faith." We sing, then, too, through our tears, the hymn that best speaks the love that sustained our father from his first encounter with Jesus, and would sustain him, and us now: "My Jesus, I love thee, I know thou art mine ..."

I will love thee in life, I will love thee in death;
And praise thee as long as thou lendest me breath;

And say, when the death dew lies cold on my brow
If ever I loved thee, my Jesus 'tis now.

————

His breathing grew shallower still, more quiet. Just little sips of
air. Marg and her husband went to get our little mother and a
nurse came in, quietly and gravely, to shut the oxygen off. The
breathing became even quieter. Our niece, Teresa, had taken
Marg's place across the bed from me. Together, she and I watched
the last, ever more widely spaced breaths. For one moment, he
raised his head from his pillow and, as though he were gathering
up all of life's light into one last gaze, his eyes focused, intent and
piercing in one last look—not at us, but at some point beyond
us, and then he lay back. Teresa, an experienced nurse, showed
me where to watch the pulse flutter, like a moth under the skin
at the side of his neck, until it stilled. And then she shut his eyes.

Dimly enough, yet somehow surely, I realized that the
same love my dad had responded to in the gospel invitation in
his youth was the love in which, and into which, he died. As
the apostle Paul puts it, "I am convinced that neither death nor
life … will be able to separate us from the love of God that is
in Christ Jesus our Lord" (Romans 8:38, 39). The new birth
my dad experienced in his late teens was just the beginning of
something; the day he died, its promise was fulfilled. In dying, I
believe my father was delivered into the full presence of the One
whom, having not seen, he had loved.

And so, seeping up through the fatigue and the sense of
huge loss, there was for me, as there had been at other birthings,
"joy unspeakable and full of glory." My dad had been born again,
again.

————

Maxine Hancock, PhD, is the author of many books, including
*Living on Less and Liking It More* and *Gold from the Fire: Postcards
from a Prairie Pilgrimage*. A recipient of the Leslie K. Tarr Award

for her outstanding contribution to Christian writing in Canada and the Leading Women Award in Communications and Media, she has appeared frequently on Vision TV and the CBC, spoken and lectured widely on matters of faith, and is professor of Interdisciplinary Studies and Spiritual Theology at Regent College, Vancouver.

# Safe in the Dark

~ *Ray Aldred* ~

It is nearly sunset when our plane departs Regina for Ottawa.
Somewhere over Brandon, Manitoba, I look out the window and
see the darkness. I have to look for a while before my eyes can
focus on the odd yard light on a farm, or an occasional town.

We humans were not made to live in the dark. We sleep in
the dark; we shut down for awhile; we come close to dying. My
wife tells me that when I sleep I sometimes stop breathing for
a moment. She waits for a second, and I always start breathing
again.

I used to go hunting with my dad. Sometimes he would take
a short walk while I waited behind in the truck. I remember
seeing him trek down a cut-line, wearing his orange-red hunting coat made out of heavy material. He was six foot six and had
wide shoulders, and he used to make me feel so safe when he
was around. Now he walked with long strides, his toes pointed
out into the spreading dusk. The trees closed behind him, leaving
me all alone.

The truck was still warm because the motor had just been
running. But as the sun went down, it seemed as if the cold came
from the dark and slowly crept in, even through the doors. I
locked the doors because all of a sudden, the dark seemed to be
hiding something. It seemed to take away my courage.

So I would sit and watch for my dad. I would wonder why
he was taking so long. It probably wasn't that long, but it seemed
long to me. What if something happened? What if he didn't come
back? All the crazy thoughts that go through your mind when
you're a kid, alone in the dark.

*What's taking so long?*

It was cooler now and the windows had a layer of mist that
added to the spreading gloom. It wasn't like the dark in my parents' wardrobe at home. We used to go inside and close the door
and sit in the dark, but we knew that it was light just outside.

But this darkness was everywhere; it seeped into every corner. It seemed to stifle everything.

My eyes moved back to the place where I had seen my dad disappear, looking, hoping he was there. Then my heart raced. I could now just barely see a movement—not like the wind or a shaking of branches, but a spot clearing where the darkness had moved out of the way. First, the top of his head, then his face, then his shoulders—my heart leaped for joy.

I wanted to get out of the truck and run and throw my arms around him and say, "Dad!" But I stayed. I just waited. Grinning, relieved. Dad stood beside the truck, scanning the four directions one last time. I was impatient now. I wanted to yell, "Get in the truck before the darkness gets in!" But he was never afraid; the darkness was nothing to him.

He opened the door and hauled his huge frame into the truck. He turned the key and the truck roared to life. He pulled out a switch on the dash and brilliant light streamed gloriously into the darkness. The darkness had to move; it was no match for my dad and me. We could move on.

"The people in darkness have seen a great light," announced Isaiah, the prophet. I don't think people were made to live in the dark.

---

Ray Aldred is a member of the Swan River Cree Nation in Alberta and assistant professor of Theology at Ambrose Seminary in Calgary, where he lives. He chairs the Aboriginal Ministries Council of the Evangelical Fellowship of Canada and is on the board of the North American Institute of Indigenous Theological Studies. An ordained minister, Ray is a contributing editor for *Cultural Encounters,* a theological journal of Multnomah Bible College, and a frequent speaker at conferences on cross-cultural ministry.

# The Voice of Silence

*~ George Whipple ~*

For those ashamed of being human
the simple rituals of nature
(the rustle of the rain,
a salmon-leap of wind
that wrinkles clouds on water)
are like a charm to summon
from the mind's thesaurus
the distant deer bells of a poem
stepping shyly through the darkness
to find its only writer.

To silence or to speech
the ear must pay attention:
the deaf relate by signs
that seem to finger-sing:
sharp hail's a language
understood by blind men.
By turning down the noise
in your head, you may find
yourself in conversation with
the novice-master's voice.

In meditation there is peace.
The outer world is stilled.
You become an ear.
You learn to listen
to the silence in the silence.
At first, with luck, you hear
the sound of distant deer bells:
and then, from even farther,
a voice that falls more softly
than footsteps on the water.

George Whipple is the author of nine books of poetry, including *The Peaceable Kingdom*, "which explores the notion of Canada as a peaceable kingdom through our mythology, culture and environment," *Footsteps on the Water*, and *Tom Thomson and Other Poems*. He was born in New Brunswick, grew up in Toronto, and now lives in Burnaby, British Columbia.

# Home
~ *Gloria Ostrem Sawai* ~

On the first Monday in November the sky darkens, the wind takes on a hollow, whistling sound, and the people of Stone Creek wait for snow. They wait in the Chinese café at oilcloth-covered tables beside steaming windows, coffee mugs cupped in their hands. They wait in the Golden West Hotel in a room dimly lit, where one more drink will warm the winter already in their bones. They wait in the Stone Creek school. Restless in their desks, the pupils twist their bodies this way and that, stretching their necks toward the high windows, watching the sky darken, deep, deeper still, now a dense heavy grey. And the wind, sharp and mournful, slapping at the glass.

And then it comes. Icy flakes spinning in the air, sweeping across the roads, under telephone wires, into ditches. It blows against the café and post office, the furniture store and under-taker's parlour and the schoolhouse windows. It swirls about the elevators and across the pasture and the quarry and over pebbles and stiff clumps of thistles and all around the empty chair creak-ing back and forth beside the frozen pit.

Inside the trailer, Nettie peers out the small window over the sink and watches the flakes do their jagged dance in her small yard. She breathes content in the knowledge that now, Eli will never leave her.

She goes into the bedroom, opens the closet door and reaches behind a pile of blankets for the package. She removes the yellowed paper, lifts out a small black autoharp, and carries it into the kitchen where Eli is sitting. She places the instrument on the table.

"Here," she says. "Play."

"Wherever did you find this?"

"Never mind. Just play."

Eli examines it, fingers the knobs to tighten the loose strings, then plucks the strings with his thumb.

"No," Nettie says. "Use this." She plunks a thick piece of worn leather into his hand."It's what Mama used." And Eli strums a few chords.

Outside, snow drifts around the trailer, clicks and swishes against the kitchen window. And the wind, blue and hollow, seeps under the door in chilly strips.

"Sing," Nettie says. And Eli opens his mouth to an old song.

*Mid pleasures and palaces, though we may roam,*
*Be it ever so humble, there's no place like home.*

"Speed it up," Nettie says. "You're too slow."

*A charm from the sky seems to hallow us there*
*Which seek through the world, is ne'er met with elsewhere.*

"Oh, well," she says.

*Home, home ...* Eli sings.

"Home!" Nettie shouts.

*Sweet sweet home ...*

"Sweet home!"

*There's no place like home,*
*oh, there's no place like home.*

Nettie sighs. "That is so true," she says.

❧

On the seventh of November Annie Levinsky dies. Jacob Ross and his pupils tromp through snow down the hill to the Russian church. Inside, they cling to the wall by the door. The church is crowded, everyone stands, there are no pews. Elizabeth Lund stays close to Mary Sorenson. She has never been in this church before and she stares at everything. In front of her, men in black suits and white shirts, women in black skirts and lace shawls, and children, too, hover around a wooden box that Elizabeth can barely see. All around them are candles. Purple candles in tall stands that rise above their heads; pink candles in little glass cups set in cubbyholes in the church wall; candles in thick silver candlesticks on the table of the altar. Hundreds of orange flames. And she sees the pictures too, painted on the walls and on velvet banners with red tassels—pictures of old men with beards and of Mary and the baby Jesus. And the ceiling! She gazes up at the blue dome high above, where saints and angels fly in and out among the stars.

Mary takes Elizabeth's hand. The two girls press closer to the varnished box. And there she is. Annie Levinsky, lying on creamy slippery cloth and wearing a long white dress. Annie with a veil fluffed around her face and holding a red rose in her hand. Her hand is stiff, her eyes are closed, she has rouge on her cheeks, she's wearing lipstick. Mrs. Levinsky is leaning over her, crying, fussing with the veil so it lies in curves around her daughter's face. And the bearded priest is swinging a purple cord with a silver cup on the end of it and chanting in a dark strange language. Smoke rises from the cup, and Elizabeth can smell spices—cloves or cinnamon. It's too much all at one time and she closes her eyes.

And now the men in black suits are carrying the box outside. They carry it to the open grave in the churchyard. And Mary and Elizabeth are standing together by a mound of frozen dirt. Again the priest chants and swings the smoking cup, and smoke rises in thin streamers into the cold grey air. With thick ropes, the men lower the box into the hole, and the people throw chunks of frozen dirt down on it, each clod landing with a thud. Then, for the first time in the entire service, the priest speaks in English. "Let us go forth as light bearers to meet the Christ who cometh forth from the grave as a Bridegroom."

Elizabeth whispers into Mary's ear, quietly but with authority, for she's the daughter of a preacher, "She marries Jesus." Then the two girls take each other by the hand and begin to cry, softly at first, only a few sniffles, then louder until they are sobbing, their bodies shaking. Weeping for Annie Levinksy whom they didn't know really, never played with, hardly spoke to, for Annie was a shy girl, sick and smelling sour. But now, oh wonder, she's the bride of Christ. And one day she'll be pulled right out of the dirt to meet her husband in the air.

Annie Levinsky, lying at the bottom of a frozen hole, wearing lipstick and a long white dress, and smelling like cinnamon.

---

Gloria Ostrem Sawai is a writer and editor. She grew up in Saskatchewan and now lives in Edmonton, Alberta. Her short story collection, *A Song for Nettie Johnson* (Coteau Books, 2001) won the Governor General's Literary Award for Fiction in 2002. Her story "The Day I Sat with Jesus on the Sundeck and a Wind Came Up and Blew My Kimono Open and He Saw My Breasts" has been widely anthologized.

# Can I Go with You?

~ *Bruce Cockburn* ~

When you ride out of the shining sky
To claim the ones who love you
Can I go with you?
Can I go with you?

When the angel shouts from the heart of the sun
And the living water flows down
Can I go with you?
Can I go with you?

When the earth and stars melt like ice in the spring
And a million voices sing praise
Can I go with you?
Can I go with you?

---

Bruce Cockburn's career as a singer-songwriter encompasses
twenty-six albums, including twenty gold and platinum records
in Canada. His numerous international awards include the Order
of Canada, the Canadian Music Hall of Fame, and the Tenco
Award for Lifetime Achievement, an Italian prize. He has performed in countless concerts around the world since he released
his first solo work in 1970.

# Permissions and Sources

TREVOR HERRIOT. "El Marahka IV" is excerpted from *Jacob's Wound: A Search for the Spirit of Wildness* by Trevor Herriot © 2004. Published by McClelland & Stewart Ltd. The book is also published in the United States by Fulcrum Publishing. Used with permission of the publishers.

MICHAEL W. HIGGINS. "On Monks, Monsters, and Manuscripts" by Michael W. Higgins is reprinted with permission from *Ten Talks Celebrating the Creative Process* (University of Waterloo Library, 2002).

SARAH KLASSEN. "Elegy for the Red River" by Sarah Klassen first appeared in *Poetry As Liturgy: An Anthology by Canadian Poets*, edited by Margo Swiss (Toronto: St. Thomas Poetry Series, 2007). Used with permission.

JOY KOGAWA. "Where Was God?" is excerpted from *The Rain Ascends* by Joy Kogawa (Penguin Canada, 1995). Reprinted with the permission of Joy Kogawa.

JAMES LONEY. "Crossing to the Other Side" is an adaptation of a talk James Loney gave August 9, 2007, at the inaugural Interfaith Summer Institute for Peace, Justice and Social Movements sponsored by Simon Fraser University in Burnaby, British Columbia.

PRESTON MANNING. "The Child in the Midst" by Preston Manning first appeared in the *Winnipeg Free Press*, December 29, 2002.

JOHN BENTLEY MAYS. An earlier version of "On Bergman" by John Bentley Mays appeared in *The Catholic Register*.

# About the Authors

*Byron Rempel-Burkholder* is an editor with Mennonite Publishing Network, working with a variety of books, periodicals, and congregational resources. He edits the inspirational magazine *Rejoice!*, co-published by MPN and Kindred Productions.

*Dora Dueck* is the author of two books: *Willie: Forever Young* and the novel *Under the Still Standing Sun*, as well as many articles, stories, and reviews. She has worked as editor in a variety of book and magazine projects, including *Sophia* magazine, and as associate editor of the *MB Herald*.

# Notes and Reflections

# Notes and Reflections

# Notes and Reflections